Advance Praise f
on D

The decline of a city should rest squarely on leadership. Healthy, growing, vibrant communities embrace a wide diversity of employers, so there's a job for everyone. The automotive industry has a strong history of providing such needed diversity to communities.

> **Dixon Thayer** - *former Vice President of Global Development, Ford Motor Co.*

We are unlikely to reach our goals if we don't have a strong business community that we work closely with. Real revitalization will almost surely require Haltom City to attract private investment.

> **Nancy Watkins** - *former Mayor Haltom City*

Most citizens are not aware of how a city operates and the importance of small businesses as a financial foundation for the community and property taxes.

> **Jan Joplin** - *Kennedale City Council, Mayor Pro Tem*

Today more than ever, a city's success is inextricably linked to a strong tax base that a healthy business community brings. There is much to be considered in this book, lessons for all who are sincerely interested in change for the better.

> **Andrew A. Jones, Jr.** - *MS, CFO, Fire Chief (Retired) City of North Richland Hills*

I fully support the authors' conclusion that if automotive uses are not permitted in the commercial corridors and a Unique Selling Proposition is not developed by the business community, residents, council and City Staff, these corridors will continue to decline.

James Pliska - *Zoning Consultant, Planning Director of Haltom City*

With the restrictive ordinances set forth by the City Council in the last few years, the city has made it harder or next to impossible for small businesses to open their doors, much less survive. Mom and Pop businesses-built Haltom City, and now they are no longer welcome.

Dewy Marcum - *Haltom City commercial property owner for 45 years. Haltom City resident for 67 years. Served on City Council from 1978-1986 & 1999-2003*

This book should be required reading for local leaders and government officials and is a blueprint to build and retain a growing, prosperous community, which will in turn abate crime.

Lee Jackson - *former President of Fort Worth Police Officers Association, Vice President of Combined Law Enforcement Agencies of Texas, National Association of Police Organizations*

The authors have many years of valuable experience to share. The book is more than informative; it contains important lessons that can help our neighborhoods, towns and cities prosper.

Jack Byno - *Haltom City Municipal Court Judge 1999-2003*

Like you and others, I believe the southern part of Haltom City offers significant economic opportunities, but at the same time, it has a negative impact on the image of the city which is an important part of economic development.

Charles Scoma - *Developer, 14 years city council member, Mayor, & member of the BISD Board of Directors in North Richland Hills*

I love this book. I read it and I think you hit the points that all of the commercial brokers have with Haltom City which has killed many of our deals. Congrats on a well written book, and I am proud of you for trying to make a difference for the residents and businesses in Haltom City.

Michael Berkowitz - *CEO, Colonial Commercial Real Estate LLC, Property Managers LLC*

I find the manuscript insightful, with little to argue with.

Bob Watkins - *Mayor Pro-Tem 2014-2017, serving on ZBA, P&Z, EDC and TIRZ*

Any city that bars new automotive businesses and makes the current one's legal non-conforming in their commercial districts simply isn't being realistic, and that applies especially to a lower income city. That policy is not in the best interest of the city, though it may pander to those that don't like automotive uses. If rules and regs are in place to prevent issues, and they are, simply enforce them (like having the cars towed). Haltom City had a brand, as an automotive mecca, and it has killed it as the city declined.

Steve McCune - *McCune Construction Funds Management LLC, serving on City of Fort Worth Urban Design Commission & Historic Preservation Commission*

Since I've been on City Council in Arlington, I've come to realize how moribund the city policies and practices are, more so than I had already guessed. Probably the same in most cities. But in a smaller city like Haltom City, it should be easier to effect change. I find it exciting that you are trying to do just that. Smaller cities have an opportunity to change direction and reinvent themselves.

Rebecca Boxall - *Registered Architect, Arlington City Council, District 5*

The authors present what all cities must grasp, that the business community and attraction of new businesses have to be a top priority to revitalizing their aging areas.

Tom Wilder - *Tarrant County District Clerk, 1995-current*

This book should be a must read for everyone fighting for the life of their city. It reinforces my view with some concrete examples of why we need more business people and fewer do-gooders and attorneys in charge!

Matt Hayes - *Business Entrepreneur, former Judge JP 7*

As a past building official, no one can appreciate the need to partner with the business community to keep the city relevant and progressive better than I can; the book is spot on.

George Patterson - *Building Official, Planning and Services (Retired), Arlington*

Ron Sturgeon and Gregory Smith have done an excellent job of shining a light on the issue of cities decline from within. It's a topic many see but few discuss or take action.

Ron and Gregory have not only pointed out the issues but offer excellent solutions. We should all pay attention!

Betsy Price – *Mayor, Fort Worth 2011-2021*

Ron has laid out a framework/structure for cities to be a success from the view of a successful entrepreneur. Carefully reading will show ways city government can best serve the community they represent.

Wade Leinaar - *Manufacturer and former Controller, Yosemite Airlines*

Keeping the Lights on Downtown
in America's Small Cities

The Critical Role Small Businesses Play in Bringing Back Jobs & Prosperity

Visit www.MakeHaltomCityGreatAgain.com
for information on the book and updates.

Gregory Smith and Ron Sturgeon

If your city has a chance for declining areas, ask current and potential candidates for council if they have read this book, and if they are committed to making the city great again by making it easier to attract and grow businesses.

Published by
Mission Possible Publishing
P.O. Box 37007
Haltom City, Texas 76117

For more information, contact Jennifer Knittel at
Jenniferk@rdsinvestments.com or
817-834-3625, Ext. 232

For reseller information including quantity discounts and bulk sales, please
contact the publisher.

ISBN: 978-0-9851112-6-7
Manufactured in the United States of America
10 9 8 7 6 5 4 3 2 1
First Edition

Dedications

To all the folks serving in thankless positions on councils and committees, and for the staff, mayor, and city managers who have constantly changing bosses and constituents and especially to those listed above that strive to be agents of change, in a bureaucratically and legally challenged environment. I can only hope to make some folks think about the issues here, and have some takeaways that help them to be more fully informed and valuable in whatever role they are in. The struggle is real.

    G.S.

To all the entrepreneurs who have ever put payroll on a credit card to keep the doors open and to all those local leaders who champion them and what they do to keep the lights on in small towns across America.

    R.S.

Credits and Acknowledgments

Writers

Gregory Smith & Ron Sturgeon with additional content by
Rebecca Boxall

Project Manager

Ron Sturgeon

Editors

Eric Anderson, Brenda Noel, Paula Thomas,
Elyse Gappa, & Gregory Smith

Cover Design

Ron Sturgeon & Keith Crabtree

Photographers

Steven Simmons & Ron Sturgeon

Photo Editor

Josh Davis

Publisher

Mission Possible Publishing

Special thanks to the dozens of friends and colleagues who
voted, edited, and advised on everything from the cover's
design to the marketing campaign.

Contents

Foreword

A foreword is generally written by someone other than the author and tells the reader why they should read the book. We chose to let some advance readers of the manuscript write mini-reviews, and they are presented here as the foreword.

******

Kudos for writing *Keeping the Lights on Downtown in America's Small Cities*. As a former Director of Planning, Building Inspections and Code Enforcement in Haltom City, I support your strategy for the city pursuing a Unique Selling Proposition (USP). Haltom City's Belknap Street and NE28th Street were designed for automotive uses about 70 years ago. Much like Route 66, Haltom City had a very vibrant automotive service boulevard. The city should stop trying to erase its historical roots and support a USP that focuses on its existing characteristics. Automotive uses are an important sales tax infill for the failure of retail services because of the pandemic.

As the authors' have pointed out, historical and cultural place identity are a strong asset in unifying the city with the existing automotive businesses along these corridors. For example, used cars are a premium now due to electronic chip shortages. RV sales have skyrocketed for people wish to travel the US by roads rather than by air. Obviously then, Haltom City's existing used car and RV lots; auto repair facilities and gas stations are doing their part to maintain the city's economy during this crisis.

I fully support the authors' conclusion that if automotive uses are not permitted in the commercial corridors and a USP is not developed by the business community, residents, council and city staff, these corridors will continue to decline.

James Pliska - *Zoning Consultant, Planning Director of Haltom City, Retired*

This book is an eye-opening summary of the impact City Council and city staff have on a city. Most citizens are not aware of how a city operates and the importance of small businesses as a financial foundation for the community and property taxes. This book gives several examples of what poor planning looks like in real time and the advantages of flexible planning. It's hard to understand why a city would turn a deaf ear to their business community. Changing a culture of negativity takes time and takes people willing to stand up and get involved. Thank the authors for standing up and getting involved.

Jan Joplin - *Kennedale City Council & Mayor Pro Tem*

A city's success is supported by a balance of its tax base between business and residential properties. A city must seek and support the business community to maintain that balance. Today more than ever, a city's success is inextricably linked to a strong tax base that a healthy business community brings. As a former public safety official, I have seen how successful cities balance their tax base between support for a strong business community, a favorable residential segment and a quality public safety component. First responders (Fire, EMS and Police), the business community, and the city leadership must all provide input to maintain that healthy balance. There is much to be considered in this book, lessons for all who are sincerely interested in change for the better.

Andrew A. Jones, Jr. - *MS, CFO, Fire Chief (Retired) City of North Richland Hills*

I love Haltom City, and I think it's important that we work hand in hand to make sure that we nurture continued development, in the older parts of town as well as the newer parts. You're totally correct about there not being a businessperson serving. We've been sorely underrepresented for a number of years. I understand the mentality of voting for your friend, however winning a city council seat isn't a personality contest. The city is a business and should be run as such. We are unlikely to reach our goals if we don't have a strong business community that we work closely with. Real revitalization will almost surely require Haltom City to attract private investment.

Nancy Watkins - *former Mayor, Haltom City*

I found the book thought provoking and it addresses a problem facing most cities over seventy years old. I believe both parts of city government (city council and city management) should be working from a common vision of what is in the best interest of the community they are serving. I do not find vision and purpose statements for the city nor statements of its core values and goals on the city web site. Without these guiding principles, it is hard to have a coordinated mission.

The closest purpose statement I find on the Haltom City web site is by the Haltom City's Economic Development Department which states it *"exists to enhance community development within the city. This includes encouraging people and businesses to relocate to Haltom City."* Although there is information regarding economic development on the North side of the city, there is little mention of plans to re-develop the South side of the city.

Like you and others, I believe the southern part of Haltom City offers significant economic opportunities, but at the same time, it has a negative impact on the image of the city which is an important part of economic development. If I were asked for recommendations as to how Haltom City should move forward in economic development, I would recommend that the City Council and City Management convene a group of individuals that represent a cross-section of the community to address this issue with them. The group would include representation from Haltom City businesses (both residents and non-resident), BISD school district, and residents. This group would draft vision and purpose statements as well as a statement on core values of the city and five-to-ten-year goals which will guide the city to becoming a city that *"encourages people and businesses to relocate to Haltom City."*

Charles Scoma - *Developer, 14-year city council member, Mayor, and member of the BISD Board of Directors in the neighboring city of North Richland Hills*

This book should be required reading for local leaders and government officials and is a blueprint to build and retain a growing, prosperous community, which will in turn abate crime.

Empty buildings and abandoned houses are breeding grounds for crimes that quickly damage a local street or an entire neighborhood. Time and again I've seen people elected to leadership positions due to their "likeability" but who have no understanding of how governments or businesses actually work. This book does a great job of explaining how businesses, city officials, and first responders can work together to build a better community, which in the end affects the crime rate. Poverty and unemployment are the breeding ground for crime. Any city that doesn't want automotive in their commercial zones just isn't being realistic.

Lee Jackson - *former President of Fort Worth Police Officers Association, Combined Law Enforcement Agencies of Texas Vice President, National Association of Police Organizations*

Ron Sturgeon and Gregory Smith have done an excellent job of shining a light on the issue of cities decline from within. It's a topic many see but few discuss or take action. Ron And Gregory have not only pointed out the issues but offer excellent solutions, we should all pay attention!

Betsy Price - *Mayor Fort Worth 2011 - 2021*

Ron, I love this book. I think you hit the points that all of the commercial brokers have with Haltom City which has killed many of our deals. I feel proud to stand next to someone like you, putting on paper what everyone would like to say but is intimidated to do given the current conditions of doing business there. Congrats on a well written book, and I am proud of you for trying to make a difference for the residents and businesses in Haltom City.

Michael Berkowitz - *CEO, Colonial Commercial Real Estate LLC, Property Managers LLC*

The authors present what all cities must grasp, that the business community and attraction of new businesses has to be a top priority to revitalizing their aging areas.

Tom Wilder - *Tarrant County District Clerk*
1995-current

Any city that bars new automotive businesses and makes the current ones legal non-conforming in their commercial districts simply isn't being realistic, and that applies especially to a lower income city. That policy is not in the best interest of the city, though it may pander to those that don't like automotive uses. If rules and regs are in place to prevent issues, and they are, simply enforce them (like having the cars towed). Haltom City had a brand, as an automotive mecca, and it has killed it as the city declined.

A large portion of the population of Haltom City (and Tarrant County) falls into lower income tiers. They require inexpensive housing and lower priced retail establishments to make ends meet. These needs must be met, and the sooner Haltom City leaders get their noses out of the air and see it, the sooner things will begin to improve. I also believe a Hispanic presence on the City Council is an element of what needs to occur. Communities like Haltom City have to be more flexible when it comes to codes and ordinances in economically challenged areas of the city.

I believe the creation of the Haltom City Small Business Alliance (like HUBA) must be formed and promoted aggressively and that over time it will strategically overcome the current problems being created by a non-business sense city council and administrative branch (city planners, code enforcement, etc.). I am proud of your genuine desire to help your city.

Rome wasn't built in a day, and neither will the correction of this problem, but it has to begin somewhere, or a bad result is inevitable!

Steve McCune - *McCune Construction Funds Management LLC, serving on City of Fort Worth Urban Design Commission and Historic Preservation Commission*

Since I've been on City Council in Arlington, I've come to realize how moribund the city policies and practices are, more so than I had already guessed. Probably the same in most cities. But in a smaller city like Haltom City, it should be easier to effect change. I find it exciting that you are trying to do just that. Smaller cities have an opportunity to change direction and reinvent themselves. They have nothing to lose and a lot to gain by thinking outside the box. Bureaucracies get stuck in ways of doing things and hold onto them even if they are not working. Due to rapid social changes, we are not likely to go back to businesses (or housing or anything else) the way we have thought of them in the past. The most open to change and nimbler cities will come out on top.

Rebecca Boxall - *Registered Architect, Arlington City Council, District 5*

As a past building official, no one can appreciate the need to partner with the business community to keep the city relevant and progressive, the book is spot on.

George Patterson - *Building Official, Planning and Services (Retired), Arlington*

The authors have many years of valuable experience to share. The book is more than informative, it contains important lessons that can help our neighborhoods, towns and cities prosper.

Jack Byno - *Haltom City Municipal Court Judge 1999-2003*

This book does not seek to blame anyone, but to accurately point out where public policy has failed the citizenry. Along the way the authors give solid solutions to help cities fight decline and blight. This book should be a must read for everyone fighting for the life of their city. It reinforces my view with some concrete examples of why we need more business people and fewer do-gooders and attorneys in charge!

Matt Hayes - *Business Entrepreneur, former Judge JP 7*

Ron has laid out a framework/structure for Cities to be a success from the view of a successful entrepreneur. Carefully reading will show ways city Government can best serve the community they represent.

Wade Leinaar - *Manufacturer and former Comptroller, Yosemite Airlines.*

This will be a great outline for community leaders to use to apply common sense and basic business acumen as it relates to how to approach new business and avoid the pitfalls that have led to environments of archaic rules with no ability for being able to make the right decisions based upon the actual circumstances.

Todd Hubbard - *SIOR Managing partner NAI Robert Lynn, annual top-ten producer*

Small businesses not only run our country, they run our city. With the restrictive ordinances set forth by the City Council in the last few years, the city has made it harder or next to impossible for small businesses to open their doors, much less survive. Mom and Pop businesses-built Haltom City, now they are no longer welcome.

Dewy Marcum - *Haltom City commercial property owner / landlord for 45 years. Haltom City resident for 67 years. Served on City Council from 1978-1986 and 1999-2003*

The decline of a city should rest squarely on leadership. It takes a strong city manager to make sure the council persons know what's best for the city, to keep personal uninformed preferences and opinions out of the decisions. Cities that chose to eliminate automotive businesses are left to their peril, as those operations are a big part of GNP and livelihood of any city. Healthy, growing, vibrant communities embrace a wide diversity of employers, so there's a job for everyone. The automotive industry has a strong history of providing such needed diversity to communities.

Dixon Thayer - *former Vice President of Global Development, Ford Motor Co.*

Ron Sturgeon and Greg Smith do an excellent job in identifying the importance of small businesses as the lifeblood of small cities. They explain in simple, no-nonsense terms why small cities should welcome automotive-related businesses and encourage competition among businesses.

Veronica Chavez Law - *Commercial Real Estate Attorney and Shareholder at Brackett & Ellis, P.C. and owner VCL Commercial Real Estate Services, LLC*

Keeping the Lights on Downtown is a concise and accurate depiction of what is going on in many of the cities in America. As a political consultant to candidates and businesspeople, I have personally witnessed much of what this book discusses. This book should be required reading for members of city council and professional leaders in our cities!

Craig Ownby - *Political Consultant and President of TX Energy Resources Series 6 & 63 Investment Certifications*

It has been a pleasure and a privilege to help on this project. It is clear that you have a passion for Haltom City. We all want our hometown to succeed, but not everyone gets off their posterior and onto their feet or spends out of their wallet to make it happen. Before I moved to Florida, I lived in Southfield, Michigan, it is a wonderful place, but success is never assured or permanent. Even when I was working 50+ hours a week and going to night school, I found time to serve on boards and commissions. I lost track of how many hundreds of hours I spent in public meetings, always in the center of the front row. We did not always agree on issues, but they all knew who I was, who was with me, and what we wanted. I wish all the best to you and the residents of Haltom City and every place in this country striving to find winning formulas for the greatest good for the greatest number.

Gregory Smith, MBA, *Author, recognized for his contributions to The Mayor's Committee for the 21st Century, organized to help avert a downgrade in the bond rating for the City of Detroit.*

Chapter 1:

The Inner City & the Natural Life Cycle of Cities

It's no secret that America's inner cities are in trouble and have been for a long time. Whether you look at big cities like Baltimore or Detroit, or small towns left behind by newer development down the road, the signs are often the same. Graffiti, broken windows, grubby properties, decrepit businesses, and deserted streets. Although experts have debated the definition of "decline", we can all agree on this much—we know it when we see it.

But what, exactly do we mean by "inner city"? Sometimes the neighborhoods in trouble are on the periphery. Sometimes they are entire suburbs. Perhaps a more useful term for purposes of our discus-

> Although experts have debated the definition of "decline", we can all agree on this much—we know it when we see it.

sion is **areas in decline**. This term can adequately describe residential neighborhoods, commercial strips, or even downtown skyscrapers in distress and we use it as well as declining inner city throughout this book.

At the outset, we should point out that there is a natural life cycle to the life of cities. They are established, they grow and thrive, and later they tend toward decay—unless people take active steps to stem and reverse the decay. Rome started as a mere village along the Tiber River, probably in the eighth century B.C., grew to an imperial city of a million people under the Caesars, fell on hard times with the onslaught of the barbarian hordes, shrank to a town of maybe ten or twenty thousand in the Dark Ages, and managed to recover to become the glorious city it is today.[1] And yes, Rome still has its slums.

A decrepit house on the main corridor in the center of Haltom City. The property owner has little incentive to improve it or tear it down and build something new, as there are so many vacancies. This is another sign of a declining inner city where no one wants to redevelop land.

In this book, we will examine the signs and causes of the problem of areas in decline with a strong focus on how to recognize the signs in time to act on them, strategies for revitalizing areas in decline, and the roles that public officials, private investors, and the public at large can play in making and keeping our cities and towns vibrant.

Having introduced a new term, areas in decline, we need to clarify what we mean. Here are a few of the signs that an area is in decline:

- Rising crime.

- A lack of employment opportunities

- An increase in graffiti, junk cars, and other signs of blight in the declining part of town

- Rents falling in the area faster or becoming cheap relative to other parts of town

- The mix of businesses shifts to things like liquor stores, pawn shops, payday loan operations, and bail bondsmen

- Investors are not building spec properties or rebuilding after a fire or tear down. (a spec property is one built with no exact tenant in mind yet)

Some, like graffiti, are leading indicators, giving us an early warning that trouble lies ahead. Others, like declining rents and increasing vacancies, are lagging indicators, confirming that the decay process is well underway.

Rather than generalize, let us focus on a particular city that exemplifies the process of growth, decline, and revitalization--Haltom City, Texas, in Tarrant County, in the Fort Worth area. With a population of over 43,000, it is the 80th largest city in Texas and ranks 905th in the US according to the 2020 census.[2] Established in 1950, it has been in existence long enough and has evolved enough to make a good case study for our purposes. It grew rapidly in the 1950s and peaked in 2016. The population is demographically and economically diverse. Within its borders are residential, commercial, and industrial areas. Nearby cities compete with it for residents and investment. In other words, a fairly typical city with no extraordinary factors to make it not comparable to many other cities.

Like many cities that size, Haltom City is a bedroom community. The commercial base within the city limits is primarily businesses that support the local population, such as merchants catering to families, automotive sales and repair, restaurants, medical and dental practices, retail bank branches, and so forth. Primary regional economic drivers like manufacturing facilities are outside its boundaries. And like many of its peers, it does have some homes and businesses that fit anyone's description of decrepit. However, for the most part, it has not become an area in decline; it just has not fallen to this level. Yet. *There are parts of Haltom City that have reached that level, partly because of deliberate efforts by past city councils to rid the area of certain kinds of businesses with no plan* to replace them with something else, and other reasons, including neglect. There are lessons to be learned from this. Perhaps city councils need to be focused on not running small businesses out of town. But we're getting ahead of ourselves.

We hope this book will help residents, business owners, city planners and managers, and civic leaders see the problems and the opportunities in a new light. We will explore the tools available to identify and address the problems early. An annual self-check snapshot survey of the health of a business community can help spot troubling trends before they get out of hand. It can help determine if it is time to make it easier to start a business in that part of town and whether or not local government is doing anything—consciously or not—to restrict the growth of a viable business community. You do not want to wait until your business community is up in arms against city hall. Or moves away.

> An annual self-check snapshot survey of the health of a business community can help spot troubling trends before they get out of hand.

Chapter 2:

COVID & Trends in Retail & Office

The COVID pandemic threw every segment of society into disarray—and small businesses in particular. As of this writing, the repercussions are still reverberating. As wave after wave of the pandemic has swept over the economy, only the smartest, most progressive cities and councils will avoid being swamped in the wake created by COVID.

We focus on small businesses because according to the US Small Business Administration,[3] they make up:

- 99.7 percent of U.S. employer firms,

- 64 percent of net new private-sector jobs.

Small businesses are the backbone of the American economy. It's true on a national scale, and it's true in your city.

Consider the impact of COVID on the retail sector. The shift from brick-and-mortar retail to online purchasing began long before COVID, but the shift has accelerated and has affected retailers one might never have considered vulnerable. Just a few years ago, it would not have occurred to most people to buy groceries or furniture online. That's something you do in person, pushing your basket down the produce lane as you select an onion or a bunch of bananas. Fear of infection changed consumer habits. Smart and adaptable businesses figured out how to get us to go online, make our purchases, and select pick-up or delivery. In a remarkably short time, COVID drove changes in consumer behavior and business operations. What remains to be seen is whether cities will adapt to the needs of businesses who feel the ground moving beneath their feet. Cities that think they can backfill all the empty buildings with retail are sadly in denial.

An abandoned retail or service business on the main corridor in Haltom City. A few decades back when these corridors were bustling centers of business, a landowner would have remodeled and rented, but there is no incentive to do so today with so many vacancies.

The office sector is another prime example. The long-standing model of the office to which workers commute is being challenged. Remote working arrangements are not new, but COVID accelerated the trend, and it has triggered a profound rethinking of how work gets done. But in the meantime, all that office space is still under lease. And even if short-term employment losses are made up, will the same buildings in their current configurations still be in demand? If not, there will be vacancies. We won't know for a while because businesses will not default on their leases except as a last resort. Typically, those leases are for five to ten years. When they mature, they will not be renewed.

From the street (or from the tax assessor's office), it may appear that nothing has changed, but it has. Unless another business needs office space set up for yesterday's needs, we can expect vacancies. Already, some businesses are trying to sublease space, but it's likely to be at below-market rates. As leases mature, rates are likely to drop, causing property taxes to drop. Business owners know this. What they don't know is whether city officials are aware and are capable of the kind of flexibility it takes to adapt to the challenges of the times.

Another consequence is lost employment. In the short term, it's not too difficult to quantify. But over the long term, the jobs may not come back, or at least to the same location in the same form. The shift in the way things are done, like the shift to online retail or the shift to work from home, will likely have long-term consequences.

Small business is likely to sense the change and adapt. The question is whether cities will adapt as well, or cling to policies that hamper entrepreneurs.

We have yet to understand how inflation will play out. It may actually make property values grow, but will cities then lower their tax rates? There are a lot of factors we just don't know yet.

The future does not have to be grim, but business-as-usual policies will not suffice to ensure a bright future. Forward-thinking leaders need to realize that it's no time to be closing businesses or making it harder for new ones to open. We need a serious public discussion about things like adapting to the trend in online commerce, how to backfill vacant spaces, how to repurpose existing buildings, how inflation rekindled by supply chains disrupted by COVID will affect our cities, and how to reverse the accelerating decline in many areas. Ron noted that one person in his city said they didn't want any more title companies. That's puzzling as such service businesses are going to be needed to backfill the vacancies left in retail.

We call on our elected officials to join business owners in a serious review of the following, as they think about

> Forward-thinking leaders need to realize that it's no time to be closing businesses or making it harder for new ones to open.

how to improve their city and if applicable, their declining inner areas:

- Consider getting all stakeholders focused on how to attract more businesses, especially in the declining corridors

Consider getting all stakeholders focused on how to attract more businesses, especially in the declining corridors

- Make sure staff, council and city management all have a mantra of what we can do to help, instead of "we can't do that"

- Consider a brand for the city

- Think about what they can do to make their city more attractive than sister cities that are likely asleep at the wheel

- Review their master plan with an eye towards how to make the city's zoning match the brand

- Make sure citizens and other stakeholders are involved in any planning meetings, and actually allow their input (In Haltom City, the mayor frequently does not let people speak or strictly limits their time to just a few minutes, even on really important topics)

- Review the use tables to make sure that it's easier for other types of businesses to open or expand. Review any processes or procedures that hamper business development

- Create overlay zones for the weaker parts of the cities, with incentives and other devices

- Think about how to attract more private capital especially in the declining areas

- Make sure that all stakeholders are at the table, including first responders, business owners, and landlords

- Develop a plan for contacting landlords of vacant buildings to advise them of things the city can help them with

- Don't close or make businesses legal non-conforming

- Look at the results outlined in this book from other cities, including a redesign of the old system of zoning and conditional use permits (CUPS) to a more relaxed paradigm that allows more administrative decisions

- This is a big, jaw dropping job, but we need to "eat the elephant one bite a time" and get started.

These actions will create more jobs close to home and shore up the business tax base so residential taxpayers will not be burdened with future tax increases. That is how together we can ensure a brighter future for all.

Chapter 3:

Decline in Inner City

Reasonable people might dispute exactly how to define urban decline. But most of us know it when we see it. Buildings falling into disrepair and decrepitude, weedy lawns and overgrown or dead landscaping, and abandoned vehicles are easy to spot. Probe a little beneath the surface and you find statistical evidence that you might have guessed at, such as declining rents, more vacancies and longer periods of vacancy, and a less prosperous demographic. Public safety statistics round out the picture with a rise in crime, more frequent incidents of fire, sometimes of suspicious origin. At some point, you reach a tipping point and anybody who has a choice will head for the exits.

An indicator hard to ignore is what the major retail chains decide to do. They have staying power to weather a downturn or two, but they also have the brainpower and experience to do their homework. By the time they decide it's time to leave, the early warning indicators have been flashing for a while.

Let's examine one such case study, CVS in Haltom City. Haltom City residents have said that they want a major grocery store ever since Kroger left some years back. Now, another location in a national chain, CVS, has left from the spot across from where the Kroger closed. These stores have long leases, so it's not readily apparent when they are doing poorly because they stay open. However, when their leases mature, underperforming stores close quickly, often with short notice. In this case, CVS is closing nine hundred stores, (three hundred per year for the next 3 years) out of their 9,900 stores, so less than ten percent are being closed. Haltom City didn't make the cut. When you're in the bottom ten percent, you need to be concerned.

Closed CVS drug store on the main corridor Haltom City. As the inner city continues its decline, the larger stores are leaving.

This really would not surprise anyone who drove down Denton Highway, given all the decrepit vacant buildings. A voluntary alliance of business owners in the city, Haltom City Business Alliance (HUBA), believes that many of Haltom City's leaders are in denial about Haltom City's declining inner city, including the central and southern older areas, and NE 28th Street. It's true that the city recently proposed a Tax Increment Reinvestment Zone (TIRZ), a 30-year plan to create a special district that allows some additional money to be used for infrastructure and public improvements only. Studies have shown that creating a TIRZ can be helpful, but many studies have concluded that private investment is needed to revitalize inner cities, and a strong relationship with the business community and attracting small business is the best and fastest way to get all the vacant buildings occupied. We believe that Haltom City's City Manager has done a great job attracting larger distribution centers to Haltom City, but those plans are not going to stimulate small business growth in the declining areas.

"Large businesses are not going to come to declining corridors, ever, and can't be incented to do so," said Joe Palmer, a spokesperson for HUBA. "They won't come until the corridors are thriving again, as they were 20

Tidy used car lot, one of few remaining after Haltom City made most car dealers legal non-conforming in 2003, making the car dealer main corridor a wasteland today.

years ago, before the city embarked on a misguided plan to limit certain kinds of businesses to beautify the city."

It was common knowledge, though forgotten today, that in 2003, Haltom City Council made most car dealers legal non-conforming, and most are now all gone, as the members of the city council intended.

Earlier this year, the current Haltom City Council made most other automotive businesses (auto repair shops, tire shops, battery stores) legal non-conforming, and they will also go away over the next decade. All but one of the current members of Haltom City Council have been outspoken about limiting the automotive business-es, but they have also made it hard on other less intense use small businesses to open, like dry cleaners and swim-ming pool accessory stores.

"Dry cleaners can't even open without public hear-ings, unless they want to be in the industrial districts of

Haltom City," said Palmer. "Dozens of other similar retail and service business types also can't open without the same conditional use permit hearings that take months and cost the owners thousands of dollars to hire consultants to complete the needed paperwork and meet the other requirements."

"The net result is that Haltom City is at a competitive disadvantage in the race with nearby communities to attract start-up small businesses because these same uses can open in surrounding cities as an approved use, paying their fees, and getting their usual inspections, and certificate of occupancy within days," noted Palmer. A recent third-party study pointed out that Haltom City had the most restrictive use matrix from all of its sister cities for many uses including automotive.

Many studies have pointed out how use tables and permit requirements prevent the growth of small businesses, and the importance of the lost commerce. Arista Strungys, AICP, with the American Planning Association noted that use regulations "…can create unintentional barriers for small businesses, businesses that have positive impacts on a community that go beyond direct economic benefits." Strungys advises cities to take care that use rules do not "…create unintended barriers instead of opening up opportunities for entrepreneurship."[4]

HUBA believes that a lack of business owners on the Haltom City Council, both in the past and currently, has limited the process of change and prevented the adopting of business-friendly ordinances. Instead, the council members have adopted a strategy of not allowing things that they personally don't like. They also fail to think of what's best for the city in the long run, instead they follow the advice of a few vocal members of the community, mistakenly thinking that those comments must represent the thoughts of all the citizens. In particular, the city has failed to recognize that the needs of residents in the central and southern parts of the city are different than the emerging modern development on the north side of the city, said Ron Sturgeon, a founding member of HUBA and owner of a real estate development company that employs 15 based in Haltom City. Also, residents fail to understand the tradeoff for their tax base. Due to rapidly increasing property values, sales tax from businesses is much smaller as a percentage of overall revenue, and it's clear to see that if sales taxes had kept up, ad valorem taxes could be lower for Haltom City's real property owners.

Strungys explains the effects of use rules like those Haltom City has this way: "Older ordinances often build inflexibility into commercial use permissions in two ways: 1) by taking a specific use approach and 2) by organizing permissions in a cumulative or pyramid system of uses. Combined, these approaches can frustrate potential new small businesses by requiring lengthy and expensive special approvals, complicating interpretations of permissions, and discouraging emerging uses. The specific use approach has become disfavored in modern practice because of its length and inability to respond to new and emerging uses."

Haltom City doesn't want automotive businesses because they aren't as compliant as desired. Ms. Strungys addresses that in her comments, "Zoning does not regulate the quality of a use or operator. This must be enforced through other regulations, such as licenses and nuisance ordinances. Sometimes residents' concerns are that they like a certain use when run by Operator A, but not Operator B. Zoning cannot make this distinction. To realize the benefits of small businesses in a community, the municipality must eliminate the roadblocks within its zoning regulations. When a zoning ordinance permits a range of uses, it can facilitate small business innovation, make it easier for small businesses to establish themselves and take root, and send a message that small businesses are welcome within the community. Then, when zoning acknowledges the physical form of small businesses and does not force standards upon them that they cannot

A tire and repair center on one of the main corridors.
These are now barred, even though the city has a low
demographic and a lot of older cars on the road.

meet, the community becomes more business friendly. By taking a look at their current ordinances and evaluating them through these lenses, communities can ensure that their zoning regulations encourage the growth of new---and the success of existing—small businesses."

We believe it would be advisable for the council to think about how to attract more small businesses, instead of limiting them, especially in these times when all cities are competing for small businesses. Haltom City could be the "prettiest girl at the dance" among Tarrant County cities if the members of our city council would adopt the appropriate strategies. The city, arguably, has more potential than most if not all of other Tarrant County cities.

HUBA has asked numerous times for the council to review the matrix of uses to make it easier for new businesses to open, and made numerous proposals for changes in sign ordinances, encouraged the city to review processes for Certificates of Occupancy, track requests by new businesses, and various other things to streamline getting more businesses in. The council has never even recognized the alliance exists. It has even submitted a set of proposed revisions to the use matrix to Haltom City Council. The city's use matrix determines whether a given type of business is permitted in various zoning classifications and whether any special conditions must be met for the business to open in an area with a particular zoning. Palmer added, "I simply don't get why any city would snub the businesses that are wanting to grow the business tax base."

Chapter 4:

The Old & New Parts of a City

Every city is unique in its own way, but a thoughtful look at the demographics of a place—its mix of ages, income levels and accumulated wealth, ethnic and racial backgrounds of its people and so forth—can be illuminating. Often, especially when the city has been in existence for a few decades or more, we find that areas within the city and the population within those areas diverge. If you were to take a snapshot of the demographics every year and line them up like scenes in a movie, you may notice that there is a natural progression. None of this is surprising and you see similar patterns in most cities. That is why Haltom City is a good case study. It's not so old or complex that we cannot observe and describe clear patterns, which can be a starting point for discussion of general urban patterns. We are confident that our readers find the same processes going on in their own cities.

Haltom City was established in 1950. The newer northern portion, generally north of Loop 820, tends to be more affluent. The older portions, generally south and central in ZIP code 76117, tend to be less so, with older homes, younger families, and more Hispanics (47% of Haltom City is Hispanic) or immigrants, with more vacant properties, and properties in need of more tender loving care. The rents are lower, so younger people and those without much money gravitate there. This is not surprising. As cities age, properties are less desirable, and don't command the higher rents that the new part of town can.

One of the few inner-city motels in Haltom City. As crime and drug use increase and these age, they attract unsavory tenants. These certainly define the old and the new parts of the city.

It is also worth noting that, not surprisingly, the newer and older areas of town have a different mix of zoning categories. This may be largely a matter of changing historical circumstance over time, but it would be prudent public policy to be cognizant of the differences. They have different needs and should be nurtured with different and appropriate policies from City Hall. But at present, the City does not explicitly recognize any differences in terms of policy. It's not surprising that council members don't like it when you "call their (policy) baby ugly." Ron says when he travels abroad with his fiancée, they always ask to go to the ghettos. Almost always, the guides say, "We have no ghettos." Almost all cities have a ghetto if they are over 50 or so years old. (Or maybe they have such a strong brand that the ghettos never came?)

We should also note that as of this writing, no Hispanics have a seat on the city council. (One Hispanic member was term limited out.) We're not postulating a cause-and-effect relationship, but it's something to ponder. As a general rule, it is helpful if political representation is closely in tune with the people represented.

There are subtle (and not so subtle) differences between the newer and older sections of town. For example, the auto mechanics in the old section may not be ASE certified, but their skills are well matched to the challenges of maintaining and repairing the aging vehicles their neighbors are likely to be driving. Again, this is not the sort of thing Nobel Prize winning economists study, but it is typical of the realities that may escape the folks at City Hall when they attempt to formulate policy for the city as a whole without realizing all of the gritty realities. City officials ought to have it as a checklist item: are there relevant differences between different sections of town that need to be considered? Are there unique circumstances in (say) a particular industrial or commercial area? Do current city policies create obstacles to private investment? It's not hard to create overlay districts and put innovative policies in place in them to spur whatever development or improvements a city wants.

We have seen it time and again. Officials just a bit out of touch with what's going on in the less advantaged parts of town dream up top-down grand strategies. The city planner goes off to a convention and sees glamorous projects reported from other cities and they want that shiny new thing as a career enhancer. Or it can be as simple as futile efforts to throw incentives to a grocery chain to build a new store in a particular neighborhood to fight blight. The corporate planners can see that it is not a good fit. They recognize the risk of building a store in a blighted area and may have had unsatisfactory experiences with exactly that approach in the past. A potential anchor tenant does not find an empty, abandoned strip attractive. They don't see it as their responsibility to lift up a blighted area. Their responsibility is to their investors to ensure the maximum return for the minimum risk.

Some cities blame landlords, saying they should be forced to rent their buildings or keep them fixed up. One thing is certain: all landlords want to rent their properties. Detractors want to "force" the landlords to rent at cheaper rates, which sounds good, and landlords are generally motivated to do that. But what do you do when, like in Haltom City, commercial realtors don't show space except as a last resort because they know that the tenants aren't going to be willing to wait months for public hearings? They simply show the space in surrounding cities where there are no such requirements. Why should you wait months to open a dry cleaner here, when you can open down the street in a week? This, of course, leaves the losing city getting their dry cleaning done in the sister city, and a vacant building. In many cases in Haltom City, centers have been vacant for years. With no prospects and no showings, the landlord is not incented to improve the center until and unless they have a real prospect. As soon as realtors realize that the city is actually allowing tenants to move in without public hearings and a minimum of paperwork, they will start showing the spaces. The city could also allow incentives with stipulations, like a façade or finish out grant of say, $25,000, if the landlord or tenants is spending at least $75,000 on improvements. Those stipulations could be in a certain area or maybe an overlay district they have created that has a lot of decrepit vacant (or occupied) buildings.

There are plenty of examples of how not to do it. Kennedale, Texas, about eleven miles from Haltom City, wanted to make the old part of town more like the newer part. What did they do to accomplish that? They spot-zoned one restaurant right in the heart of the industrial zone (clearly in violation of their master plan), between a cement plant and a junkyard. It might have worked had there been a demonstrated customer base within the work forces of those two businesses, but nobody but the planners at City Hall saw that pent-up demand. However, no tenant stepped forward to endorse that as a great idea. The result was a complete failure. And their economic development corporation bought select properties so they could hold them and only sell or lease to a tenant they liked. Trouble is, they still own them ten years later. And since cities have seemingly unlimited funds with little accountability, Kennedale decided after one of those fancy development conventions that they needed a Town Center. "Build it and they will come" isn't generally true in commercial real estate. A private investor would never risk such an endeavor without lining up tenants first. And no lender would finance it without tenants. The city can sell bonds, build it then wait. Then wait some more. Then rent at below market rates to finally get SOME tenants. They don't have debt service covenants like regular investors. Most people don't even know they've passed the Town Center, as it is a horrible design. And the taxpayers likely have no idea that it cost over $10 million, and is still burning money with the low rent rates and weak occupancy. When it doesn't rent fast enough or well enough, the solution for Kennedale was obvious. They decided it needed to be larger, so they build more. The citizens have no idea how many millions have and are being spent to prop up something that will never be widely accepted.

Conclusion

If you want to turn the tide in an area on the skids, the answer comes in the form of small businesses attracted one at a time by individual landlords who get the lights back on and can make improvements to the property as they fill it with tenants. Business logic, not grand strategies dreamt up in city hall, provides the driving force behind rejuvenating business districts. City hall can assist or just get out of the way, but it cannot dictate the details. To do otherwise is to risk wasted time, resources, and opportunity.

There are strategies that city hall can pursue to reverse the trend.

1. Develop and promote a clear brand for the city—a clear idea of what your city is, what makes it distinct from others, and what it encourages—to attract new businesses and retain current businesses. If you are not familiar with marketing strategy, consider this: if you say Coke or flash the familiar logo, sweet liquid refreshment and a certain lifestyle comes to mind. That didn't happen by accident. This is what the Coca Cola marketing people say: *"For 125 years, we have been refreshing the world."*[5]

Simple and powerful. Your city needs to do that too. And those fine folks at city hall will need professional help to do it. There is a reason marketing professionals make a lot of money. Don't try to do it on the cheap. Make it mean something. Not "A lovely community," or "the best place to live." Competent small business consultants encourage clients to come up with a unique selling proposition (USP). Usually they say things like "we give the best service," or "we have the best product."

They actually think that because they say it that makes it true. Nothing could be further from the truth. You have to say what makes you better and what are the benefits to the customer. What do you measure to make sure you are fulfilling your promise in that USP? Author Ron Sturgeon loves to measure and wrote a book on metrics and benchmarking to help his clients understand their power. According to Bob Watkins, Haltom City once had a good motto, "Proud and Progressive", and they changed it to "A Place to Call Home". Bob and many others believe the prior motto was much better and actually meant something. One thing is certain, if a city decides to *really* make a change in its brand, it should change the motto to convey that as part of the rebranding. Also, as part of any rebranding, a marketing budget and plan should be established. If, for instance, Haltom City modified its use tables to lower the barrier to entry for businesses, and allowed automotive, those changes need to be announced and marketing, which could bring meaningful results quickly, certainly within a few years, as realtors started showing space and business inquiries were hearing yes instead of no. In the last 60 days, I have had calls from at least 3 interested prospects that were told no for some type of use, and the city staff they wanted retail in that space. Counting on retail to populate the vacant buildings is a terrible strategy. As outlined in a later chapter, the population is growing faster in 75% of the cities in Tarrant County than Haltom city. The city has continued to fall in the rankings, according to census records, so no, not many are calling it "a place to call home".

2. **To bolster a failing business district, try a brand-based overlay district.** You will need the active support of business owners to do this. You can't just dream it up and push it through by majority vote of the council. This is why it's good to have an ongoing dialog with your local business alliance. Don't just talk at them. Listen to them. Work with them.

3. **Don't do anything that makes it harder for businesses to grow.** And don't take actions that are going to close anything but the most intense businesses, like sexually oriented businesses. The rules of commerce will bring you what you want. As long as council seats and boards don't have any prior business owners serving, the city is at a disadvantage attracting new businesses.

> Don't do anything that makes it harder for businesses to grow.

4. **Determine in advance how you will measure your progress.** How many new businesses have opened? How

many have you lost? In both cases, find out why. Listen closely to what the owners have to say. Use an annual checklist survey to tally wins and losses. How many vacant buildings, and how many square feet are vacant on a given day each year?

5. **Benchmark similar cities elsewhere.** Yes, your city is unique, but others face similar challenges. What are the winners doing right? What mistakes do you see others making? What is the big picture?

All of this takes vision, determination, and some strong business ownership experience. Folks without it, often retired with the time to serve in this thankless job, have the best of intentions, but they often struggle unless there is a business owner or two on the council.

Chapter 5:

Who's in Charge

You've got to respect the people who serve on city councils. Almost without exception, they are honest, hardworking folks who want to serve their community to make it better. In your area, they may be called aldermen, commissioners, trustees, or something else, but we are talking about legislators—people who adopt by majority vote the rules (ordinances and codes) that affect your life. It is often a thankless job.

The median salary for a council member in the US is $20,500 per year.[6] In smaller cities and towns, there is no salary. Instead, they may be

In your area, they may be called aldermen, commissioners, trustees, or something else, but we are talking about legislators—people who adopt by majority vote the rules (ordinances and codes) that affect your life.

paid by the meeting, often a nominal fee, like twenty-five or fifty bucks.

They attend long meetings and listen to the concerns—and grousing—of their constituents. As public figures, they may not be able to get through the grocery store without being stopped by somebody who wants to talk about city business with them. They learn not to put frozen goods in their basket until they are ready to get in line for the cashier. At any point, 51% of the constituents are for something, and 49% are against. Or worse, a very high percentage are just apathetic.

Who are they and how did they wind up serving on a city council? For starters, unless we are talking about big cities, council pay and the hours filter out anybody who needs to work full time or anyone who has compelling demands on their time. It can be very difficult to get time off for civic duties if you work for a major corporation. Unless you are in a big city, the job does not pay enough for you to quit your day job and make it your main occupation. And besides, your term is up in a few years, and you must run for election again, so you might be out on the street. It is simply too risky for most to make it a full-time job. That's why you find a lot of retirees on city councils.

What kind of background do council members have? Where, professionally speaking, do they come from? The answer is just about anywhere. In their lives before entering public life, they might have been school teachers, employees of local companies, corporate managers, just about anything—with a few exceptions. Arguably, if the council could run like the business, it is, applicants would need to be qualified, vetted, reviewed, and interviewed. Only those qualified would be considered. But because it's such a thankless job, and especially in smaller cities, it's hard to get anyone to run. That isn't meant to be negative or pejorative about those that do, they have a genuine desire to serve and they do the best job they can. Unfortunately, they don't know what they don't know, and many times simply don't have the skills or experience associated with running a business. The decisions can be hard and complex.

Local business owners tend to be too busy operating their own enterprises to have the spare time for running for office. And many of them, perhaps the really smart ones, are wary of potential conflicts of interest. A business owner serving on the city council can—and indeed must—recuse himself from voting on any matter that even remotely appears to be a conflict of interest. Some cities are being more innovative. Kennedale, a small enclave in Texas, recently passed an ordinance that allows business or property owners that *don't live in the city* to serve in a non-voting role on their Economic Development Committee. This is a good decision because it brings more stakeholders to the table and shows local leaders are interested in the concerns of members of the local business community. Cities should consider allowing property or business owners to serve in one seat on all boards and as elected officials. Most small cities don't have a lot of competition for such seats, and this would bring a lot of knowledge to the panels. It's what a board of directors brings to a company, levels or fields of expertise. Imagine, for instance, a city council with no prior real estate experience being asking to approve a multi-year lease in a city owned property, or an agreement to build a town center, like Kennedale did. So only members with no real estate experience and the city's lawyers handle everything. This simply can't be the best plan, as none of the parties knows that they don't know.

How do you learn how to be a council member? Is there a school for it? Generally, no. Some associations, such as the Florida League of Cities, have orientation sessions for newly elected council members. They cover things like the general requirements of the state constitution, public records laws, avoiding conflicts of interests, things like that. In other words, how to avoid getting fined or sued, and staying out of jail. But you won't find much help on topics like dealing with contractors, roads and traffic management, water systems engineering, labor relations, zoning, city planning and growth management, or any of the nuts-and-bolts skills you need to manage a city day-to-day. Most of the limited training is about legal issues, don't do's, and social media use. Again, someone in that community is, for instance, a zoning expert, but they can't serve since they live outside the city. Or what about that restauranteur that has opened a dozen restaurants, maybe in other cities. Nope, he can't serve either. Does everyone agree that he knows what new restauranteurs look for in a city before considering opening a new eating establishment?

So, who does the day-to-day nuts and bolts tasks? The city or town has a staff. In a very small town, it might be a single person, the town clerk, who answers the phone, pays the bills, takes minutes and types them up, and a hundred other things it takes to run the town and follow the rules laid down by the state constitution and statute. It's a big job and in small towns, it doesn't generally pay all that well. So, if you have a competent and energetic clerk, count your blessings and make sure that person's pay is in line with the local market, or you will spend a lot of time searching for and training replacements. Remember, even in the public sector, free market economy rules are in operation. Small towns hire contract attorneys and planners.

As you go up in size, a town starts taking on specialized staffers. First, you need a lawyer, whether your town has a retainer arrangement with somebody with expertise in small government matters, or big enough to have one or three in-house. (Yes, I said first. After all, this is America, the most litigious country on earth.) Second, you need someone to manage the books and maintain public records. Then, depending on a variety of factors, you need public works people, police and fire, trash collection, building code management, code enforcement and, if your city is big, a horde of specialists you can only guess at. And once you have all those people, you need a city manager to ride herd on them, and city managers are paid well. City manager base salaries average almost $92,000 per year. Don't forget that averages can mask the extremes. Some city managers make over $170,000 per year.[7] Anybody drawing a salary like that may also qualify for performance incentives, so keep that calculator handy. Maybe they deserve all that money. After all, they have as many bosses as you have seats on the city council, and oh, by the way, their bosses change every few years, and they've got all the citizens in their ear as well.

All those department heads reporting to the city manager have professional staff. The city engineer probably has an engineering degree and maybe some professional engineers reporting to him. The city finance director specializes in government accounting practices (and yes, those practices differ from garden-variety business practices, but that's a subject for another book). The public works director has his own area of expertise in moving people, equipment, and dirt around. Then there is the police chief and the fire chief and their departments. We are talking about more staff, all of whom report to council members.

Or do they? She comes to the regular meetings prepared to do her bit to make her city better, but that meeting packet can get complicated. The city manager and his assistants come to the mic and report, request, recommend, and, well, generally advise local elected officials. If a new councilperson is worldly wise and has some spine, she may urge her fellow council members to think for themselves and tell the staff to go back and work out more choices on the issue at hand. But often, if the issue is complicated, she and her colleagues will accept the menu of choices presented. A or B. Accept or reject an application or project request. Grant or deny a variance. She is relying on their expertise and judgment more and more.

This is democracy at the grass roots, right? But here's the rub. Jane Q. Retiree (and she has the biggest heart and honest to a fault) may never have owned a business, or at least one of any scale or consequence—and neither have the staffers. You have people running a city who have never met a payroll (and certainly not out of their own pocket), never dealt with OSHA, never had to do a lot of things that any business owner does every day. Ron notes that he doesn't think a single councilperson in his city has ever filed a plat or applied for a conditional use permit and presented that at public hearings. But they all say they don't think requiring a CUP and public hearing impedes small business development. Members of the business community may propose projects that stand or fall on the numbers to make them work. So, if a business owner submits a plan that requires, say, a curb cut for an entrance at a particular place along the highway, or a certain minimum number of parking places, or place-ment on a particular parcel of land to be redeveloped, the council person may just go along with the staff recom-mendation. Or she may throw a wrench into the works and demand changes that make no business sense.

For example, we witnessed a proposed event center for a properly zoned vacant property. The event center would provide a venue for things like weddings, graduation parties, festivals, things like that. The plan involved food trucks to sell food. City staff seemed to be on board with the plan. However, individual council members wanted to get into details, such as how many sinks were required in each truck. We will assume that those members felt they were doing their due diligence and protecting the public, but that detail is managed at the county level. Also, in most cases, unless there are health or safety issues, the council shouldn't be meddling in a business plan of the operator. The council even issued a rule on where the trash generated would be disposed of – outside of the city. The plan, which had been carefully researched and prepared at considerable expense was, after multiple hearings, dropped. The result? A vacant property remained unused and opportunities for constructive economic activity was squandered for another six months until the persistent applicant applied again and got a better result.

Here is another example of misguided effort borne of lack of business sense: many cities have vacant industrial space. The sensible thing to do would be to recognize what they have, promote and incentivize an industrial storage zone. In one instance, Kennedale wanted to do away with industrial uses, even though the master plan showed it as the intended use. What did the council want to do? They wanted a concert venue there. Really?

Nobody's going to come to concerts there. If you look at where any of the leading hospitality companies build their new hotels and motels, you will not find them in industrial storage zones, especially next to a junkyard. Hope is not a business strategy.

Many city councils tend to have a lot of newcomers. Many cities have a city council that has four first-term members out of seven seats in any given year. How many of them have a deep understanding of the challenges facing the city, much less the problems facing business owners? How many have specialized experience, say, negotiating with a cell tower company? That leads us to another perennial challenge: lack of institutional memory. Not only do you have people with no business experience trying to impose their nonexistent business judgment on the community at large, but the newcomers keep trying things that failed in the past. Why? No idea what has been tried before and either worked or flopped.

Let us turn our attention to city staff. They tend to have more longevity, so they have fewer excuses. If you poll the business community, you may find they frequently have unfavorable impressions of city staff. Why? Indifference. Arrogance. A sense that if they are here to serve, it's not to serve you. We understand that they must balance different constituencies, but why can't they see business owners as an important part of the community? Things might be different if the city manager told each of his department heads, "I am going to invite comments from our community about how well you are doing your job in their eyes. And every time I get a complaint, you and I are going to have a meeting and you are going to explain to me why that person in our community is unhappy with you."

What a wonderful opportunity to make your city different. Have you ever noticed how many businesses talk about the quality or focus of their service, but how few actually do it? Ron defined a term in his book of business jargon, *Green Weenies and Due Diligence.* The fish rots from the head. If the city manager and the council really want the city to be business friendly, the staff will find a way to deliver on that. In a few years, the city will have a Unique Selling Proposition, USP, and will be known for its friendly and pragmatic practices. That city will for sure be a happier place to be, for everyone, including all the employees.

Wouldn't it be nice if when you wanted to put up a fence that was 6" too tall, city staff told you it wasn't allowed by code, but they found an exception in chapter 6 subsection 4 if the fence was stained and not painted. Also, in the city we've just described, the staff are much more likely to make an administrative decision to allow something (because they can, and it's encouraged), whereas in most cities making a decision is not incented.

We watched as council in Haltom City turned down a snow cone stand because they said it had to be regulated like a food truck. It was pointed out that they could treat it as a restaurant and it would be allowed, but that fell on deaf ears. Or the large trucking company that was operating legally for decades but cited because the city found out that they had mechanics to work on their own trucks, and their property was not zoned for truck repair. I know, you're shaking your head in disbelief, just like we did when we found out about it. Maybe it's time to rethink the fish's head, and instill a new mantra of just serving and being happy?

Why doesn't this happen? In part, because the city manager is insulated. He knows that it takes four out of five council members to fire him. It takes a lot of complaints from the public to get the city council seriously upset with him. It's a challenge in these bureaucratic times we live in to make such changes, and you could be demonized for just making the suggestion.

The challenge is to help elected officials and city staffers understand free-market economics and how business owners think.

In any case, it's up to the city manager and the council to make their city the prettiest girl at the dance, and then love life. It's easy to say, hard to do. The challenge is to help elected officials and city staffers understand free-market economics and how business owners think. That is what this book is all about.

Chapter 6:

Understanding the Table of Uses & CUPs

Have you ever driven through a run-down section of town and asked yourself how things got this bad? Perhaps it's a section of town that was thriving when you were younger, and you remember it when it was new and had that sparkle of prosperity and optimism. What happened?

Private enterprise is a key factor in the health of our cities and towns, in fact, the driving force. Our popu-

An older vacant strip center. The main corridors have lots of these in Haltom City, as in many other cities with declining inner cities. Realtors say they seldom show such properties.

lation centers thrive where and when there is vigorous trade and commerce, and they wither and decline when businesses die off. The prime mover in either case is the power of individuals making business decisions. Stay, and maybe expand? Hold on, but don't invest further? Or give up, cut your losses, and try somewhere else? In the case of sole proprietors, an individual is placing a bet with his own money that he or she can do well in this spot. In the case of a corporation, a person or group of people are making that decision on behalf of investors. In either case, someone is trying to make a profit doing business in that spot.

> Our population centers thrive where and when there is vigorous trade and commerce, and they wither and decline when businesses die off.

But private investors don't make those decisions free of constraints. Over time, society collectively saw the wisdom in setting some rules about what goes where. We can all agree that a lead smelter should not be next door to the kindergarten. A pig farm should not be in the middle of a residential area. Lead smelters and pig farms are necessary and valuable parts of our economy, but common sense tells us that everybody is better off with some rules.

The first zoning regulations in the United States were established in 1908. By 1920, the US Commerce Department formulated model codes that could be adopted by the states and local governments.[8] In some areas, they are called land use codes. The general idea is to group compatible uses together and to keep incompatible uses separated by some reasonable distance. The main points to remember here are that they are designed to prevent the creation of nuisances and they have the force of law. They protect people and businesses already established from the introduction of incompatible uses, and they offer guidance to anyone considering establishing a new business. It's better to know up front that what you have in mind will create a problem, generate complaints, and result in adverse legal action.

One concise way to specify what can go where is a use table, a matrix that plots defined categories like commercial and industrial along one axis, and types of business activities along another. Intensity of use may be differentiated from light to heavy, so C-1 can designate simple retail zoning (think mom-and-pop establishments) all the way to C-5, like a car dealership. (C means commercial, M means industrial, as in M-1 and M-2, M-2 being the heaviest industrial)

Within the matrix, at the intersection of a defined category and a business activity type is a code designating what is allowed or not. The codes may designate allowed, prohibited, permitted, conditional use permit, or special exception. The matrix is used in conjunction with a land use (or zoning) map which assigns categories to every piece of land within the jurisdiction of the city or town.

We offer the Haltom City, Texas use table and zoning map[9] as an example.

So far, so good. It all seems perfectly reasonable. You have an idea for your business, you do your homework and work out a business plan, and you go to city hall to fill out the forms and write a check to cover reasonable fees. And there is where it can all start to go sideways.

What exactly do we mean by "conditional use"? For definitions, we consult Section 36 of the Haltom City Code of Ordinances.

The purpose of the conditional use procedure is to allow for review of uses which would not be appropriate generally or without certain restrictions throughout a zoning district, but which, if controlled as to the number, area, location, or relation to the neighborhood would promote the health, safety, and welfare of the community. The procedure is intended to allow broad public review and evaluation of the proposed development and to ensure adequate mitigation of potentially unfavorable impacts.[10]

A reasonable person may think good! A little flexibility with an opportunity for public oversight and comment.

From a business owner's perspective, let's remember a few things. Time is money. And frankly, money is money. At some point, filling out forms, submitting architectural and engineering drawings, time waiting for answers from city staff people and so forth goes from being just something we know has to be done to being an unreasonable burden. If you have to pay a lawyer or other professional to prepare the application, those people don't work cheaply. Delays and mounting costs can eventually undermine the business case for a project. A rational business owner may decide it's just too much trouble and risk.

A less obvious but no less important nuance is embedded in that bland, legislative language: "...if controlled as to the number, area, location or relation to the neighborhood..." Think about that for a minute. Put on your free market cap. Who should decide "the number, area, location, or relationship to the neighborhood" of a new business? An entrepreneur who has studied the market and is willing to put his money into a new venture? Or a city official who may know little or nothing about the market and who risks little or nothing with a decision to approve or deny the request? By what criteria should a city official decide how many stores or dry cleaners or optometrists should be within the city limits. Or where they should be?

But one might argue, city officials have a duty to act in the public interest. What would happen if there were too many of a particular type of business? What would happen is that either they would all do just fine, or the weakest one might be unable to compete, leaving the market to the best, the strongest, the most adaptable, the one most preferred by customers. How would a government official ever be able to anticipate the best outcome?

The short answer is that government does not know. It has been tried. Centralized economies with government functionaries allocating resources were a dismal failure as the people in communist societies discovered. However, it does open the possibility for anticompetitive meddling. If a merchant or group of merchants fear the arrival of a new competitor, all kinds of reasonable sounding objections can be raised—parking, traffic, whatever—and the government official with the authority to approve or deny a permit may find the objections persuasive. It's hard to see how a busybody mayor or city council has much to contribute to what should be a straightforward business decision.

The meddling does not stop there. If business operations are suspended for a period, for instance if the owner suffers a health crisis or a fire, the conditional use permit may be terminated. Couple that with an onerous applica-

A tidy quick oil change business. These are barred in all the commercial districts in Haltom City and must have public hearings and a CUP to start up even in the heavy industrial district. Businesses like these are staples, especially in a low demographic city. When and if this property goes empty, with its automotive design construction, it is likely to stay vacant forever. In a more vibrant corridor, it might be torn down, but land is available and not many new buildings are going up in those corridors.

tion process and you have an environment unfriendly, if not downright hostile, to businesses.

Unclear definitions create more difficulties. The Code of Ordinances makes no distinction between a dry-cleaning plant with all those chemicals regulated by the EPA and a storefront establishment that only serves as a drop off and pick up point. For some reason, Haltom City seems to disfavor businesses selling swimming pool accessories. They have banished automotive related businesses from commercial zones, relegating them to industrial areas only. Consumers don't want to go into the industrial area, next to the concrete plant or large manufacturer to get an oil change, a new set of tires or to have paint and body work. An even more extreme example is the case of a proposed event center. The project required a small mountain of application paperwork, duly completed, and four public hearings over a span of two months. Members of the public unknown to the applicant got up and spoke out in favor of the project. Yet one council member insisted on getting into the minute details, such as how many sinks are required in the food trucks that would operate at each event (a matter regulated by the county), or how many would be allowed at one time, or whether a city police cruiser should be required at each event. It was proposed that those food trucks would not be allowed to dispose of their waste within the city limits. We will charitably assume that the honorable council member was just trying to do her homework, but the net effect was that after a lot of delay and unnecessary expense, the applicant dropped the project and the people missed out on the chance to enjoy a new service. Bob Watkins, a local resident who has attended virtually every council meeting in the last 20+ years commented to me after one of the meetings that he had never seen an issue get so far into the weeds, especially since the county regulates and registers food trucks, treating them just like restaurants. It's a great example of a city council that is not focused on bringing business and has a bias to micro manage every applicant.

> Elected officials have the responsibility to balance the needs of the business community and the desires of residents.

These are just a few examples, symptoms of the problem. We can all agree that elected officials have the responsibility to balance the needs of the business community and the desires of residents. But where they strike that balance can make the difference between a thriving city with a strong business tax base and a city where business is not welcome.

Chapter 7:

Infrastructure & the Limits of TIRZs

Infrastructure is one of those topics that makes most people's eyes glaze over—until there is a problem that affects them personally. Let's face it. You have to be a public works nerd to get excited about water supply systems, drain system capacity, sewage treatment, traffic studies, or dozens of other snoozers. In this chapter, we discuss the declining inner city, and the challenges cities face there with infrastructure. Another fact that everyone agrees on, it's expensive, and with falling taxes in the decrepit parts of town, where will the limited money be allocated?

But as soon as residents and business owners find themselves on the wrong end of a chokepoint like their street or access blocked, they get agitated. And who could blame them? Isn't somebody supposed to be planning and managing all that?

Just to keep things clear, we need to distinguish between public and privately owned infrastructure. Roadways, water supply systems, drainage and sewerage are commonly (but not always) owned by cities, counties, the state, or the federal government. Alterations to what is there now has to be planned and negotiated. However, electric power distribution and telecommunications facilities are usually owned by investor-owned companies. They have different legal and engineering groups and practices, but guess what? Once again, alterations to what is there now has to be planned and negotiated. The upshot of all this is that everything, no matter how minor it might seem to you, has to be planned, applied for, permitted, and paid for, even if it's just getting a curb cut for a parking lot or moving a pole. And it has to be factored into your timeline. That's why good project managers are well paid.

You incur significant expense even before the first step in erecting profit-making structures like stores, apartments, etc. In addition, you have to coordinate with the owners' things like electric utilities, cable and telecommunications, etc. If you want it done next week and they tell you it's more like six months, you'd better plan on six months – or perhaps a year. And don't forget, they own easements and right-of-way all over the place. You need to research that and work around things like that.

From the discussion above, it should be clear that development is expensive and brownfield redevelopment is even more expensive. Another thing is clear to everyone, declining inner cities usually have infrastructure issues. So, who pays for what? What if redevelopment costs become such a barrier as to dissuade investors? When it is in the public interest to stimulate redevelopment and to encourage private investors, a local jurisdiction may create a Tax Increment Reinvestment Zone. Many cities have just such a provision in their municipal code:

1. **TIRZ** - Tax Increment Reinvestment Zones (TIRZs) are special zones created by city council to attract new investment in an area. It's important to note that these usually have long lives, 20-30 years, and take several years to get going. What is most important about this discussion as it pertains to declining inner cities, is that the TIRZ can only help with public improvements. Need a sidewalk? You could be in luck. What it won't pay for, is fixing up any personal property, including decrepit buildings. It's important because many studies have shown that public money simply isn't enough, it takes private money to save an inner city. These zones help finance costs of redevelopment and promote growth in areas that would otherwise not attract sufficient market development in a timely manner. Taxes attributable to new improvements

> Tax Increment Reinvestment Zones (TIRZs) are special zones created by city council to attract new investment in an area.

(tax increments) are set aside in a fund to finance public improvements within the boundaries of the zone.

2. **TIRZ Board** - The Tax Increment Reinvestment Zone (TIRZ) Board will make recommendations to the city council concerning the administration, management, and operation of the designated reinvestment zone. The board is delegated by the city council all powers necessary to implement any project and finance plan approved by the city council, including the power to employ consultants and enter into agreements that the Board considers necessary or convenient to implement the project and finance plan and to administer, operate, and manage the reinvestment zone including, but not limited to, the power to enter into reimbursement agreements and other obligations secured by the TIRZ fund established in the TIRZ ordinance. Many cities want business people on such a board, especially those with development and construction experience.[11]

Conclusion

These zones are complex, and as you can imagine, require a lot of knowledge, paperwork, and experience to utilize. They are only one tool in the box for helping with revitalization efforts. Usually, they are used by large, sophisticated developers as they know how to maneuver the paperwork. When it can cost millions just to build sidewalks, it's easy to see that a TIRZ could be used for one development here and one there, every few years.

Does your city have 30 years to stop the decline, relying on public money? It seems unlikely for most cities. Bob Watkins, a 25+ year resident of Haltom City is cautiously optimistic about the proposed 30-year TIRZ the city is putting in place, but notes "I was the Chair of the TIRZ in the northern part of Haltom City for nearly five years [some years back] and we were handed A 20-year TIRZ to live with. We never met, therefore accomplished nothing."

The bottom line is that a thriving city depends on a thriving and diverse business community offering products and services for customers within the city and from the surrounding areas, and employment for people in the area. Economic activity—people buying and selling goods and services—is the foundation of wealth and a powerful force driving increasing business real estate value. That supports healthy tax revenue streams which in turn pays for city services, helps fund infrastructure, and pays city employees. It is either a virtuous circle, raising all boats, or a vicious cycle, sucking everybody down. Without a thriving small business community in the failing parts of town, it is going to be a tough job to

> Economic activity—people buying and selling goods and services—is the foundation of wealth and a powerful force driving increasing business real estate value.

revitalize things. Ideally, studies have shown that a partnership with business is a requirement for success.

We need dedicated and well-informed civic leaders willing to work with business owners to make it work for everybody.

Chapter 8:

What a Strong Business Tax Base Means for Your Taxes

Let's start with the observation that government does not generate wealth. It collects money in the form of taxes and fees and uses those funds to provide services and the physical assets needed to provide those services, like roads, sewer systems, police and fire stations, libraries, and so forth.

Now let's consider the sources and types of taxes. Taxes and fees are paid by businesses, residents, and people passing through or conducting certain transactions. The tax might be proportional to the value of the property (ad valorem taxes), a percentage of a transaction (sales taxes or income taxes), or a flat fee, like a few bucks to park in a municipal parking structure or use that boat ramp we mentioned.

It may come as a surprise that generally, on a dollar-for-dollar basis, residential properties contribute less

Many buildings were purpose-built for automotive uses prior to the new ordinance, so this new huge complex, which is just what cities love and will generate tens of thousands of dollars in ad valorem taxes, now will have to have public hearings every time they lease a space. Many prospects just won't go through the process. This leads to slow lease up or reduced rents, neither of which both bodes well for new development. This discourages investment when cities make new ordinances that adversely affect previously built buildings and businesses.

to total taxes collected than businesses, relative to the expense they generate in terms of services delivered to them. Or to look at it the other way around, businesses consume less in city services than residential properties for the same dollar contributed. So, it stands to reason that it is wise policy to avoid encumbering business owners with unhelpful burdens. Bob Watkins, who I interviewed for the book, as he reflected on Haltom City's slow downturn said, "it sometimes seems that elected officials stay up nights deciding what they can throw into the mix to make it nearly impossible for business owners to survive, never mind prosper."

Writing for the Amarillo Economic Development website, Doug Nelson observes that "Expanding the economic activity within a community is one of the primary goals of every elected body, community Chamber of Commerce, Economic Development Corp., and business professional. The stronger and more diverse the economy, the stronger the community becomes. Over time, a strong economy becomes a self-sustaining engine of growth that can help bolster property values and add 'curb appeal' to an entire region."[12]

One of the impetuses for co-authoring this book, Ron Sturgeon ran into the city buzz saw when he wanted to open a new business, where he started his first of many businesses fifty years ago. He formed a business alliance to work on making the city business friendly and was instantly demonized. The fact that a business alliance forms with such a stated goal is a real indication of an issue. The fact that HUBA was ignored just shows how insular a city can be to change. In a forward-thinking progressive city, a business alliance interested in interacting to bring more business would be welcome. And it would certainly seem to be the right kind of seed to plant to spur private investment when businesses are willing to participate in improving the city.

This is one of those things that can work as a virtuous or vicious circle, depending on whether it's working in your favor. One way to keep it going in your favor is to make sure your business tax base is diversified, which is a fancy way of saying you don't want all your eggs in one basket. To the extent that the various parts of your tax base depend on different businesses that are not completely linked to the same economic forces, when one industry is in a downturn, the others may be less affected. For example, light manufacturing might hit the skids in a recession, but a strong banking sector might be doing just fine. On the other hand, if all or most of the businesses in your tax base are tightly bound together in a single industry, they will tend to rise or fall together. If the economy catches cold, your city may get pneumonia.

Nelson concludes, "Consequently, these cities are less appealing for new businesses seeking to open their doors. Industrial diversification provides protection against complete collapse. This also helps protect the tax base, which means that the community's civic services such as police, schools, fire departments, etc. don't have to curtail service or offerings. This provides stability that helps communities attract both residents and entrepreneurs eager to see the community grow stronger.

"Effective diversification requires having a balanced mix of small, medium, and large sized businesses. It also means strategically attracting businesses that not only meet the needs of today's economy but are anticipating the needs of the economy in the future. Thus, it's important to continually adjust strategy so that the economy grows in a healthy and solid direction not only today, but 5, 10, 20 years down the road."[13] The point we are making here is that the diversification should be made by entre-

> It's a common misconception that expanding the tax base is a code phrase for raising taxes. Quite the opposite is true.

preneurs applying business logic to the situation, not by bureaucrats making rules.

Nelson goes on to say, "It's a common misconception that expanding the tax base is a code phrase for raising taxes. Quite the opposite is true. When a tax base expands, it means that businesses and members within the community share in the costs associated with running the community. The larger the tax base grows as a result of increased sales, the smaller the individual's share of the tax burden becomes. This leaves more money in the pockets of community residents and business owners. As a result families, individuals, [sic] and businesses are able to purchase more goods and services that sustain the community, and give it a solid and steady rate of growth."[14]

This is not lost on businesspeople looking for healthy places to expand their operations. Cities with strong, diverse tax bases are attractive to potential newcomers because the synergies already present will work to the advantage of newcomers. They are more likely to experience robust and consistent sales, better city services, and healthier prospects for the long haul. They are less likely to find themselves surrounded by failing businesses or neighbors heading for the exits, leaving the remainder with a heavier tax burden to cover the city's fixed and semi-variable costs.

It is also true that cities (or counties or states) where the tax base is large, diverse, and healthy are less likely to have to resort to offering tax incentives to attract new business. In a paper in the Journal of Economic Perspectives, researchers report that "While we find some evidence of direct employment gains from attracting a firm, we do not find strong evidence that firm-specific tax incentives increase broader economic growth at the state and local level."[15] The authors documented an average growth of roughly 1,500 jobs within the specific industry of each deal. They didn't, however, see strong evidence of job growth in other industries or an effect on county-wide employment. If your business tax is healthy enough, there is less reason to resort to incentives to attract newcomers. They decide to set up operations in your jurisdiction based on the merits of the existing situation, not tax incentives of uncertain efficiency.

The inverse is also true. The narrower and less diverse the business tax base, the greater the risk for newcomers as well as incumbent businesses.

Often city leaders are tempted to offer incentives to large, high-profile businesses like Amazon. Size matters, but in surprising ways. Writing in Governing.com, authors Janis Bowdler and Kim Zeuli report that "Small businesses are the backbone of urban economies: They play a critical role in creating jobs for local residents. Yet too often city leaders and economic developers are not prioritizing small businesses when allocating resources to drive growth, focusing their strategies instead on the attraction and retention of large businesses."[16]

They cite a new report by the Initiative for a Competitive Inner City that finds that:

- "In four of the five cities, small businesses create most of the jobs: 58 percent in Chicago, 53 percent in Detroit, 74 percent in Los Angeles and 62 percent in D.C. In Dallas, small businesses provide slightly less than half of all jobs. Although 'micro' businesses (those with one to five employees) make up the largest share of businesses in the cities ICIC studied, medium-sized businesses (those with five to 249 employees) are driving job creation.

- The importance of small business jobs is greater in the inner city. In four of the five cities, small businesses create a greater share of jobs in distressed inner-city neighborhoods than in the city overall: 70 percent in Chicago, 64 percent in Detroit, 77 percent in Los Angeles and 74 percent in D.C. Dallas is distinct in that large businesses employ more inner-city residents than small businesses, which only account for 38 percent of jobs. [note the reference to distressed inner-city neighborhoods, the topic of this book.]

- Inner-city unemployment is not insurmountable, and small businesses can play a key role in creating opportunities."

Bowdler and Zeuli maintain that "City leaders will need to leverage new tools to maximize small-business job creation in their cities. ICIC offers five critical strategies:

- Create a comprehensive small business plan connected to regional and city economic assets.

- Expand contracting opportunities for small businesses so that they can compete on procurement contracts with government and anchor institutions.

- Design workforce programs for small businesses, since many do not have the resources or capacity to recruit and train new employees (especially those with barriers to employment).

- Coordinate resources and ease burdensome regulations by mapping and making more accessible the resources that already exist.

- Upgrade the inner-city business environment by improving infrastructure and neighborhood amenities to support small-business growth."

And above all, don't take actions that close, reduce or restrict businesses, new or existing, except for those that are risks to crime, safety and health.

Given all of the above, any intelligent person would have to recognize the stunning folly of banishing an entire category of business with deep roots in the community. Yet in 2003, the Haltom City Council did exactly that by rezoning automotive related businesses, leaving many of them in legal non-conforming status. Most of the council doesn't really comprehend the total effects or

A tidy older tire shop in Haltom City. These are now barred in commercial zones and are legal non-conforming. The city wants to limit competition and believes that the council, rather than the economics of commerce should determine how many of a given type of business is allowed.

are in denial. There is no good reason to make a business legal non-conforming unless you want it closed. Such a business is injured, often critically because:

- They are not allowed to expand, and in many cases improve their business

- If the business is destroyed, it cannot be rebuilt.

- The status casts a cloud on any sale of the business, and really who wants to own a business that the city wants closed?

- The property owner is injured, as future uses of their property are limited. In the case of an automotive business, the building is likely suited to that use, so future uses are hard to find

- The property taxes are likely to be reduced as rents fall or the property falls vacant

- The business personal property taxes are likely to fall, as the business stops growing

- If the property falls vacant for a period (usually six months), it can never be used for that use again.

Closing down businesses can be a necessary evil, but it's critical that a plan to "backfill" the vacant properties is put in place. In Haltom City's situation, no plan was put in place, and the city got just what it asked for. A vacant corridor, almost all the car dealers are gone almost 20 years later. And almost all the buildings are vacant, and very run down. Also, the lots previously occupied by the dealers, which was almost certainly the highest and best use, were very small, and cannot be developed to current

A large retail center in Haltom City. It was remodeled many years ago by the landlord but is still vacant. Another good opportunity for an indoor self-storage or some other creative use. Unfortunately, most of these uses would require a CUP and public hearings to be considered for a certificate of occupancy. One investor considered adapting it for indoor antique car storage, but he was told no.

standards. There is a lot, with a small building for an office, but no place for setbacks, landscaping, parking, and other items required by the current code. To add insult to injury, the city recently put a TIRZ in place to revitalize portions of the city, but didn't include the decrepit corridor, which most everyone agrees is an eyesore.

Recently the city made most all automotive businesses legal non-conforming, with only one council person questioning the action and voting no. The council does not like automotive businesses. Over the next twenty years, many of those buildings will go dark.

Ron tells a story of when he was working at Ford Motor Co. after he sold his business to them. There was a downturn in sales and profits, and the new CEO of the subsidiary was scrambling to increase profits, or stem losses. He issued a mandate – "Do not do anything that could reduce sales without my express permission." Now there's a novel idea.

What if cities could be friendly to business and as an added part of that plan, think carefully before doing anything that could cause us to lose businesses or miss new opportunities to get them to open in our city. Tax rates on city residents could come down as property values and business tax revenues increased.

Chapter 9:

Cities Need a Brand

We aren't used to thinking of cities as having a brand the way a business or a product does. Coke is a brand. Ford is a brand. McDonalds is a brand. The visual symbols summon up in people's minds images and motivation that drive behavior. But Haltom City? That's just where people live and work. Right? So, what is a brand? What does it mean for a city to have a brand? And how do you go about building and promoting one? And much like a product, shouldn't a city have a unique selling proposition (USP)?

Thinking like a businessperson, shouldn't we want to attract families and businesses, and have the best schools and restaurants? Isn't that the way we stay relevant with a great future, and strong tax base? In this chapter we explore why having a brand is key to a competitive edge (yes even cities should be competitive), and even more so in this post-COVID world where the pool of prospective businesses has shrunk. A brand appeals to citizens, and all the pieces mixed together provide for a great community with world-class schools, exceptional first responders, and a strong business community.

A brand helps people identify a company, product, or individual.[17] It's what sets that company or product or individual apart from all others. It's what gives them a competitive edge against the crowd, an edge that is difficult to duplicate. Just as a company wants to be the first thing a customer or potential customer thinks of, so should a city. Remember, residents and business enterprises are deciding all the time whether to move or stay put. Your city's brand has got to be something that drives people's choices, something they sense, whether or not they can explicitly define it.

A particularly clear and straightforward explanation of the process of branding a place is offered by TBPO, The Brand Place Observer, a consulting company specializing in the field. We will quote their work extensively because they offer the clearest explanations of the goals and process of place branding that we have found in our research.

First, we need to address the deceptively simple sounding concept of place identity. TPBO defines it as "the unique distinctive characteristics that exist in a place and its culture at a given place in time[18] ...historical, cultural, economic, political. They exist in people's minds and people may not be explicitly aware of them.

A related concept is that of place image. Place image can be defined as the total set of impressions that a visitor has of a particular place or reputation. The image is based on tangible and psychological characteristics uniquely associated with a specific location. The perceived image creates an attitude towards a place, a perception of quality or feeling of satisfaction and, consequently, maybe an intention to visit."[19] A variety of methods are used to create a reliably balance picture of how visitors and non-visitors see the city. The studies are also conducted according to the intent of the city commissioning the work. Are you trying to attract tourists, business investors, or new residents of a particular sort? It makes a difference, but for our purposes, we don't have to get too far into the details. Suffice it to say that the place image the study seeks to identify is how various publics see your city. Leaders have to "bake the pie" and sometimes make hard decisions, which won't always give everyone everything they want.

TBPO considers another concept—projected place image—which helps you understand what people are saying about your city. It could be anything from word of mouth or what is said about you online to references in tourist magazines or websites, public relations campaigns, news reports and articles, and so forth. Some are short-lived, others may stick, particularly negative references.[20] Think of phrases "rust belt town" or "murder city." That stuff sticks and you might not be able to counter it easily. Tools like web monitoring and content analysis can help you keep an eye on it all.

The most important task in defining the brand identity is to "formulate authentic brand values that create a sense of belonging and purpose; authenticity; consistency and sensory appeal" according to TPBO. As an example, they note that "the US reflects values of freedom, consumerism, and nation brand values include human place; real people; challenger spirit; and original thinking." The job of the brand manager is to translate those into things like pictures, symbols, language, slogans, icons, and other elements that reinforce the brand in the eyes of the relevant stakeholders, such as the people and businesses you are trying to attract and retain.

This is only a brief overview. A city's brand needs to be focused in terms appropriate to various stakeholders, such as potential business investors, residents, or institutions. All of the elements of the brand need to be presented in a coherent way. It takes a lot of thought and planning.

TPBO makes it clear that effective implementation is critical. Branding cannot be based on communication alone; it requires actual product development as well. In other words, you need to think of your city as a product capable of meeting the needs of those in your target markets. For example, if you wish to market your city as an attractive place for young professionals, you need to provide the amenities they prize—night life, cultural venues and experiences, university-level institutes of higher learning, shopping commensurate with their tastes, income, and so forth. If you are trying to attract the high-tech employers that those same young professionals will gravitate to, you will need the infrastructure that makes it possible, including flexible commercial and institutional buildings, communications gear to support multi-Gigabit per second communications, and an educated work force. You will need first-class transportation access. You will need support services like financial institutions and medical facilities and healthcare, as good as or better than the cities you are competing with. This is the product you need to offer. As you see, it's more than a nice slogan plastered on a monument sign at the city limits.

Haltom City used to be known as an automobile mecca, bustling with commercial activity. It is fair to say that the city was known for automotive uses. But the city decided they wanted all the car dealers gone, so they ran them off by making them legal non-conforming. They also passed an ordinance that said a garage or body shop couldn't exist along with a dealer's license, which instantly made many of them legal non-conforming. Proponents say that doesn't run them off, but with time as they close or new uses come or both, small scale car dealers aren't allowed to come back. It took twenty years, but almost all are gone. Recently the city did the same thing with the rest of the automotive uses, making them legal non-conforming. It's hard to imagine that most will be here in twenty years. All that is fine, but as Coke found out, you don't change the product without talking to the customer when they introduced a "new" Coke. Another way to think of it is this: "Don't change the dog food without checking with the dog." Unfortunately, the city did not make any plans for how to backfill the vacant streets and even today doesn't have a plan for the wasteland it created. Also, as a lower demographic city, where cars are a big part of life, they continue to limit all automotive businesses and make it hard for new businesses to open. They require a conditional use permit with public hearings to open a dry cleaner. Does a city need protection from dry cleaners? Ten years behind the curve, after much hand-wringing and public hearings, they recently started allowing food trucks in the city, albeit with rules and only in certain areas. Again, do resi-

A newer retail center stands vacant in Haltom City. It's in a commercial zone, but a dry cleaner is allowed only in an industrial district. To open there, must get a CUP with two months of public hearings. An auto parts or accessory store would be a good use, but again, isn't allowed.

dents really need protection from food trucks? The city is 47% Hispanic, but not a single Hispanic person has a seat on the council. It appears that all council members are middle class, which may make it easier to overlook the "poor side of town."

In the meantime, the inner city continues to decline, while the northern new-developing part of the city gets lots of attention and new homes and businesses. It's hard not to believe that the city is asleep at the wheel and that is the inspiration behind this book.

> Wouldn't it be nice if cities could spot these trends in advance, and make plans to avoid the inner city's decline? Everyone agrees that revitalizing an inner city is an extremely hard task, likely much harder than just keeping it alive.

Wouldn't it be nice if cities could spot these trends in advance, and make plans to avoid the inner city's decline? Everyone agrees that revitalizing an inner city is an extremely hard task, likely much harder than just keeping it alive. Also, it takes capital to do either, so why not get started on it early when it is arguably less expensive, and here is the real key: Get all the stakeholders on the same page, as other cities have done, and begin a meaningful attempt at revitalization that could be as successful as those of other cities talked about elsewhere in this book, like Cleveland did, which we discuss in another chapter.

Chapter 10:

A Success Story: Midtown Cleveland

The challenges facing our cities have gotten close attention by economists, political scientists, and urban planners. We want to make sure we are focused on solutions. They are much harder to find than problems. Other cities have tried and failed to revive their inner cities, but some have found success. We haven't tackled it in this book as it is well-researched elsewhere, but a big issue with declining inner cities is housing. We believe that a strong business community working in unison with the city, other stakeholders, and private investment can play a key role in solving housing issues.

It was not easy, but the MidTown Cleveland revitalization strategies this chapter explores achieved measurable success.

It was not easy, but the MidTown Cleveland revitalization strategies this chapter explores achieved measurable success, including double-digit increases in commercial and industrial real estate, a rise in reinvestment activity that resulted in $500 million primarily in private sector financing, 425 new companies, 400 expansion or construction projects, 6,000 jobs retained and 5,500 new jobs from expansion or relocation.[21]

Michael Porter published an influential article in the Harvard Business Review, *The Competitive Advantage of the Inner City*,[22] in which he noted the chronic failure of traditional approaches to remedying the problems of urban poverty and the "crippling social problems, such as drug abuse and crime." According to Porter, "The question we should be asking is how inner-city-based businesses and nearby employment opportunities for inner city residents can proliferate and grow." He goes on to say that "We must stop trying to cure the inner city's problems by perpetually increasing social investment and hoping for economic activity to follow." We agree wholeheartedly with this statement. "Instead, an economic model must begin with the premise that inner city businesses should be profitable and positioned to compete on a regional, national, and even international scale. The cornerstone of such a model is to identify and exploit the competitive advantages of inner cities that will translate into truly profitable businesses." Porter cites examples of companies that either succeeded or failed on the basis of whether they found and capitalized on unique competitive advantage related to circumstances inherent in their inner-city circumstances. We love the glass-half-full premise, and positive attitude for working to solve the issues, instead of just considering it all the status quo. Cities across America are dragging their feet and failing to think about and then make a plan to solve their declining inner cities. Sadly, many cities aren't that concerned (though they say they are) because their revenues aren't down materially, and they have a growing vibrant part of town which is much more fun to think about and work on. Porter makes this point about clusters:

> "The competitive advantage of a location does not usually arise in isolated companies, but in clusters of companies—in other words, in companies that are in the same industry or otherwise linked together through customer, supplier, or similar relationships...

> "If locations (and the events of history) give rise to clusters, it is clusters that drive economic development."

Considering this, why would civic leaders defy business logic and drive out a cluster of existing, functional, profitable businesses, such as automotive service companies in Haltom City? There is no reason, except 1) they don't like them, or 2) they can be ugly (which is why they don't like them.) Again, the council and code enforcement are confused about managing growth vs managing existing businesses. But full stop, this is a leadership issue. We believe code compliance in this city is top notch, but can only do what they are told and need to be fully

An Asian shopping center. The Asians are the second largest ethnic group in Haltom City and have done a good job bringing small businesses in. They are very focused on the neighborhood and work together.

informed. When everyone including the city manager gets on the same mantra, business growth, that's what they will get!

The prestigious Brookings Institute, a nonprofit public policy organization devoted to solving problems facing society at the local, national and global level, published a paper titled *A Private Sector Model for Rebuilding Inner-city Competitiveness: Lessons from MidTown Cleveland.*[23] Author Margaret Murphy cites an approach known as "community capitalism" led by the private sector that "can be applied to our inner cities to create both 'profitable growth and improved societal conditions.'" Unlike previous government-initiated efforts that injected public funds (like TIRZ public funds) into various projects hoping to see results, the Cleveland experience is centered on "a nonprofit, business-driven inner-city initiative that has succeeded in creating an economic climate for reinvestment, business growth and job creation within an older inner-city commercial and industrial area." The article acknowledged that the MidTown effort was influenced by Porter's article and describes the factors driving the success of the 15-year effort, specifically, the four key elements of a competitiveness strategy that emerged from the launch, growth and success of MidTown Cleveland:

1. **Develop strong community leadership and an organization.** MidTown Cleveland is a one square-mile, 55-block area just east of downtown Cleveland. In the early 1980s, it was primarily an industrial and commercial zone, with about 400 businesses, 13,000 employees, 570 property owners and 3000 residents. It was also an area undermined by business flight, vacant buildings, crime, vice and blight.

Following a six-month feasibility study, 46 MidTown corporate, small business and institutional leaders decided to incorporate to address the area's problems. MidTown stakeholders created a non-profit organization to deal with the issues that concerned them directly: security, neighborhood appearance, public image, the productive use of land and buildings, and the development of a cohesive business community. Strategies were divided into short- and long-term plans, while modest goals were set and achieved to build confidence and capacity. [24]

Bottom line for most cities? Instead of demonizing those that want to see change, enlist and embrace them in the effort to facilitate the change. There is a lot of brain power in those small business owners. Ron's city council where his businesses and some properties are have made it clear that if you don't live in the city, you aren't important and don't even get a seat at the table. You won't get two extra seconds to speak at a public hearing, and they will impose rules to even keep you from speaking. When they have workshops, they don't even allow the public to interact, so all they get to hear is each other, and they don't know what they don't know. Another city, Kennedale, recently added non-voting property or business owners to their Economic Development Committee after years of a tumultuous relationship with the business community and citizens. It's important to note that to get to this point Kennedale had to rout prior council members that were resistant to change and transparency, and then fired the city manager. Many times, as in Haltom City's case, the current council includes well-intentioned, sincere, and hardworking people, but they simply don't have any meaningful business experience and so aren't able to make the right decisions on behalf of the entire city. Unfortunately, there are always "fans" of the current people, because they are such good people. It's a huge disconnect when cities don't think their businesses should have a seat at the table.

2. **Shape a competitive market environment in the inner-city**. Porter and others argue that inner cities are located in what should be economically valuable areas

and that, as a result, they can offer a competitive edge to companies that benefit from proximity to downtown business districts. However, in the early 1980s, many MidTown companies needed compelling reasons to remain in the inner city. The pull of safer, cleaner and greener areas had taken its toll not only on individual businesses, but on the entire neighborhood. Inner-city competitiveness involves much more than strategic location. Making inner cities truly competitive with their suburban neighbors requires attention to practical realities and changes in governance. MidTown businesses rallied around a shared commitment and strategy to make their community safe, clean, attractive, marketable and profitable. They worked with the city police to keep businesses and sidewalks—and therefore, employees and customers—safe. They defined an agenda for physical development and sought state and federal grants and loans for a land banking project that would make central city brownfields more competitive with suburban greenfield. A successful strategy emerged that laid the foundation for MidTown to become a truly competitive metropolitan location for existing and new businesses.

Haltom City is on the record repeatedly with their mantra, they don't want too many competitive businesses. Their reasoning? That too many businesses competing will create too much competition and then the business will fail. Because the city council has no business ownership experience, they don't realize that most small business founders are keenly aware of the marketplace, the customers, and all the competitive issues before they open their doors They should be, they are investing their own money! His city doesn't want any more tire and wheel shops or oil change places because the council believes there are too many. Their argument would fail if you asked them if they wanted a restaurant row, of course. The truth is that the economics of business will determine when tire stores stop opening. It's a low-demographic city, with a bustling newly developing part of town, and it might make sense to be more restrictive on tire shops in those parts, but what about in the declining inner city, where the lowest demographics are, and of course, all the older cars. It is easier for them to think about the city as one than to recognize there is a declining inner city that has different needs. Haltom City's council people *really* believe that they can control commerce and competition again because of their lack of business ownership experience.

3. **Market the location and other assets.** To make MidTown competitive, the organization adopted a marketing strategy to change the public's perception of the area. MidTown's 3-part marketing strategy included: public relations, communications, and community building to publicize the area's strengths, promote the area to targeted markets, sponsor events to enhance community cohesion, celebrate accomplishments, and keep the membership and community well-informed.

Haltom United Business Alliance (HUBA) has offered to help applicants for variances, certificates of occupancy, and to meet with those that simply inquire. That seems like every city's dream, but it wasn't even considered by the council, who sees any such activity as just trying to line the pockets of the businesses.

4. **Develop a targeted job creation strategy.** Community capitalism asserts that businesses need to be involved at all stages of local employment programs, so that businesses' needs are met and people obtain good jobs. It also insists that the economic revitalization of commercial industrial areas should be used to benefit nearby impoverished areas. Since 1986, MidTown's employers have provided a critical link between residents and jobs through a Job Match Program. At times this has been a challenge: as the Job Match Program shifted, under the Empowerment Zone program, from fitting the needs of employers to meeting the needs of the chronically unemployed, participation by small businesses dropped.

The Cleveland MidTown experience demonstrates what can be accomplished when private enterprise is allowed to lead—with the cooperation of local government.

Writing in *Grist*, the online nonprofit magazine devoted to sustainable solutions to social problems, author Brentin Mock observes:

> "'The Cleveland Model' is a gradually developing example of what that kind of supply-side investment

looks like. The city of Cleveland leveraged public, private and philanthropic funds about five years ago to launch the Evergreen Cooperative Initiative, a cluster of worker co-op businesses developed to do business with the universities and hospitals. So far, Evergreen has kickstarted a laundry service, a solar energy company, and a hydroponic vegetable farm. Naturally, they have contracts with Case Western University and the medical centers to wash staff clothing, provide electricity, and supply their cafeterias.

"Since they're worker cooperatives, employees earn [an] ownership slice in the companies after a certain period of time on the job. The goal is for each worker to develop from entry-level work skills to managerial and executive, and then hopefully branch off to start their own businesses."[25]

Haltom City doesn't have a university or hospital within its city boundaries, but they are within the region. Innovation would bring more small businesses to serve those in other cities. Now that's a competitive triumph!

The studies and articles outlined above demonstrate the crucial role that private enterprise (especially small business) plays in the health of the community. When the health of the business community begins to fail, the cure is not ham-fisted government intervention or regulatory obstacles, but creativity and encouragement of the talent pool and resources within the community itself. It is hard to imagine a situation where more small businesses aren't good things, bringing products, services, and jobs.

Chapter 11:

Private Money: A Key Ingredient to Successful Revitalization

Imagine that you're, say thirty years old and just starting your career. You and your significant other are considering moving your residence. Perhaps you've outgrown the house you now live in and are ready for a change, or you have a new job. You have a few criteria in mind, like how close you want to be to work or church or family. The distances you have in mind take in several towns, so you go for a weekend drive, just looking. The first town you visit seems to have tree-lined streets full of neat houses, and a local school with nice landscaping out front and a well-tended playground and athletic fields. You drive down the main street and see a supermarket, a pharmacy, a few restaurants and coffee shops, a smart-looking auto repair and tire shop, a bank, a few antique shops, a couple of churches and so forth. Across from the post office is a park with a white gazebo, some benches, and beds of flowers. You note a young mother pushing a baby carriage and an elderly couple walking a spaniel on a leash. The place is not wildly upscale, but it looks solid, even prosperous. You make a mental note to investigate that town further. Of course, you have budgets and know you will have to trade some amenities because of that. You are shocked at how much houses cost, and rents are the highest you've ever seen.

You follow the main highway a few more miles and enter a second town. A supermarket has a large "For Lease" sign in front. From the looks of it, that sign has been there for quite some time. A few other shops are boarded up and tagged with graffiti. You notice a strip mall with a bail bondsman, a pawn shop, a payday loan establishment, and a tattoo parlor. Across the street is a buy-here/pay-here auto lot that also rents fancy wheels. You never heard of renting wheels before and you certainly wouldn't want *those* wheels on *your* vehicle. Somebody is selling household goods in the parking lot of a closed store. You decide that you've seen enough, but as you drive past a dilapidated diner, the residential neighborhood doesn't look too promising either. The weeds along the curb, the car up on blocks in the front yard, and the shacky looking houses tell you all you need to know. The guy in his undershirt, drinking a beer on the front porch completes the picture. Again, you make a mental note— to stay away.

You could call it *"A Tale of Two Cities"* but Charles Dickens has already claimed that one. But we've all made similar observations and experienced the same reactions to places. It should not surprise us that business owners and corporate managers make the same comparisons when they look for potential new locations. They do more statistical research and may have a more defined method than the average individual, but they are making the same judgments that lead to the same decisions—to either move in and set up shop or to move on or move out if they have a lease that was signed in better times.

Haltom City has hired engineering firms or others several times to write a plan on how to revitalize the aging corridors. Twenty years have passed, and almost nothing has been done. The plans all shared two common strategies:

1. They involved public money, which as you can imagine, is in short supply

2. They had no partnership with the business community, and specifically did not look at how they might make it easier to open a business.

Many older cities have that dynamic going on within its own city limits, and misguided land use policies passed by the City Council in 2003 have made the problem worse, not better. As we examine in this book, they sought to upgrade the mix of businesses existing at the time by driving out viable automobile dealers, and limiting repair shops and body shops that did not meet their notion of the kind of businesses they would like to see in town. Perhaps those tire shops, repair establishments, and parts retailers did not meet the esthetic standards of the politicians on the Council at the time, but they met the more demanding standards of the market—they brought buyers and sellers together, generating jobs and valuable economic activity. One has to wonder why code compliance allowed then or now businesses to become so ugly and non-compliant. Insightful encouragement and intelligently crafted incentives might have led to more satisfactory results. Ron loves mom and pop businesses, and it's no secret that he includes automotive businesses in that mix. He rarely has issues with a city. Why? Because every month his property manager drives to every business park and puts "MOVE OR WILL BE TOWED" stickers on the nonoperational, vehicles or anything

A neat new building. An investor has been tearing down old houses in the commercial corridors and building these. He has vowed to never build another one, because they are suited for automotive uses with large roll-up doors. The Haltom City Council recently passed a new ordinance that made all such automotive businesses legal non-conforming. His prospect base is reduced dramatically, and arguably his building has now lost value.

stored outside that isn't supposed to be there. Two days later the tow trucks arrive. He laughs, as he actually only tows a dozen cars a year, because all the tenants know what will inevitably happen, and the stickers on cars get them moving to cure their issue. There is simply no reason that cities can't allow automotive businesses, so long as code enforcement prods them to stay compliant. He does add that it's a never-ending job.

We will pass on the temptation to ascribe motivations to the Council. But we think what was missing was the insight to ask, "What's in it for me?" from the viewpoint of a business owner and from that of a resident. The resident and the owners of those automotive businesses were comfortable with the existing arrangements and might have been happy with policies designed to help them flourish. It is unfortunate that it did not play out that way. So, let's attempt a fresh start and ask ourselves what would work for the people in that part of town.

A resident or potential resident will consider the availability and convenience of goods and services in the town and vicinity. How far do I have to drive for groceries? Can I gas up and get my car serviced near my home? How safe do I feel parking, walking, and shopping? What is the range of choices for the things I want and need? Can I find a job in my town?

Business owners or corporate scouts are looking for a location package that promises a return on investment over some predetermined threshold with minimum risk and aggravation. Factored into that decision are questions like the strength of the local market (demographics, household income, propensity to spend), availability of local labor, potential security issues, and so forth.

Writing for the Federal Reserve Bank of Saint Louis, Christopher H. Wheeler published an article "Businesses Don't Just Choose a City, They Choose a Specific Neighborhood."[26] Wheeler is a senior financial economist in the Retail Credit Risk Analysis Division within the Economics Department of the Office of the Comptroller of the Currency. He observes that "Economic activity within metropolitan areas in the United States tends to be distributed unevenly. Within nearly any city, there are neighborhoods that grow-attracting businesses that provide jobs, goods and services-and there are those that do not." He then poses a provocative question: "Why are some neighborhoods more conducive to economic development than others?"

The article examines the geography of economic activity in cities, proximity to people, local population characteristics, and proximity to other businesses, among other factors. He concludes that "One fundamental result from this study is that different types of employers tend to seek different environments. The types of businesses that do well in densely populated or highly educated neighborhoods, for example, tend to be quite different from those that seek areas with less activity and lower levels of education. As such, a plan to target development for, say, a traditional downtown area should involve a completely different set of employers than a plan to develop a suburban neighborhood." [27]

Many cities are like Haltom City, with an aging part of town and the new shiny part of town. Different policies for each aren't out of line, but for sure there should be policies that make the older part of town easier to start a business in. Few in Haltom City, would argue that the south part of town is what's in decline, and most would agree that the main corridors in Haltom City, those new residents and businesses might look at, are in those areas. In fact, Ron believes that nonresidents likely don't even think the newer part of the legal city limits are even in Haltom City, they think it's in neighboring cities.

> Many cities are like Haltom City, with an aging part of town and the new shiny part of town. Different policies for each aren't out of line, but for sure there should be policies that make the older part of town easier to start a business in.

With this in mind, we hope that city officials will take a fresh look, set aside ideas that have not worked, and give the free market a chance to do its work without interference. The first step, as we emphasize throughout the book, is in recognizing that one part of the city is different than the other, and that it's time to get to work revitalizing the older part.

Chapter 12:

Police Officers & Firefighters & the Prosperity Agenda

First responders—police, fire, EMT professionals—occupy a special place in our communities and in the imagination of the public. In healthy communities, they can be held in high esteem, as almost heroic figures. They also play a critical role in helping to identify the declining inner city, and in helping to revitalize them. Typically, first responders are represented by strong unions or associations with negotiating power. Rank and file members may be strongly influenced by their union leaders and sometimes political action committees formed to advance their agendas.

> A strong tax base enables cities to pay market rates for police and fire department salaries, equipment, and facilities.

A strong tax base enables cities to pay market rates for police and fire department salaries, equipment, and facilities. Cities unable to pay market rate for salaries and provide the best equipment possible spend a lot of time and money training public safety professionals only to see them move away to other jurisdictions when they get a few years of experience under their belts. As a result, there is more turnover, more time and money spent on recruiting, and a less experienced work force. A strong business community and tax base will help to assure that Haltom City continues to be able to pay its first responders a competitive wage. Currently, according to the websites of the cities shown, the starting salaries for firefighters are:

- Haltom City $62,221

- North Richland Hills $60,761

- Fort Worth $58,430

- Richland Hills $55,262

- Keller $59,754

The Haltom United Business Alliance (HUBA) favors paying the Haltom City's first responders as well as, or better than, those of neighboring cities for this reason. They fill a vital role in protecting Haltom City citizens and their homes and places of business. Those in favor of a vibrant small business community should be strong supporters of local police and fire fighters. HUBA supported the new law enforcement center in Haltom City because local police deserve a first-rate facility. The first responders are stakeholders, just like the businesses, and

CVS announced it was closing 300 of its underperforming stores out of 9,900. Haltom City's CVS on Denton Highway was in that group. The Kroger nearby closed a few years back.

should always have a seat at the table. HUBA promotes building a stronger business tax base to allow for the expenses related to these initiatives.

By the same token, members of local police and firefighters' unions should favor policies that help build the community's business tax base and reduce the number of vacant commercial properties in town because doing so is good for the community and reduces the risk to firefighters and law enforcement officers as they go about their daily work. Vacant buildings invite crime and are frequent targets for vandals, vagrants and arsonists. We are glad to hear Jason Steele, president of the Haltom City Fire PAC, say on Facebook in December 2021 that "Haltom City has been 'in decline' for decades."[31]

Jayson Steele
It's been "in decline" for decades. Amazingly the automotive businesses that have dominated the area for 30 years didn't stop that decline. Now more automotive businesses are the answer to stop the decline in areas where automotive businesses dominated the landscape and didn't stop the decline. Makes sense to only one person.

3d   Like   Reply   4 ☺

What firemen know is what they see on the streets everyday and they don't see the need for one more automotive repair shop. The goal of bringing more businesses to the city is a given. Bringing the businesses our citizens want and need are the challenge.

Admitting there is a problem is the first step towards finding a solution. Small businesses have been closing, but the big stores are leaving also. CVS is closing 300 of their under-performing stores this year out of 9,900. Haltom City made the list. Crime was rumored as a factor which is consistent with increased crime in the declining inner city. Few groups have as compelling a long-term interest in promoting new small businesses in the community as fire fighters and patrol officers. The business alliance in Haltom City was surprised when the fireman's PAC was against policies to bring more businesses to the city, and especially when their president said that the firemen did not want more automotive businesses. It is always unfortunate when all the stakeholders aren't pro-small business and that hinders the city rising to the next level of innovation and change and slows the growth of the business tax base.

Closed Kroger grocery store in Haltom City. The city did attract a discount store to part of the Kroger center, which is a good fit for a low demographic city, but the city seems oblivious to the fact that brick and mortar retail is for the most part gone. Many cities would be rezoning and looking for alternate uses. A large indoor self-storage could be a good use but isn't an allowed use in Haltom City.

A solid, happy first responder group is critical to rebuilding the inner city, just like a vibrant business community. Neither likes decrepit boarded up buildings, so their goals should be the same – recognize that there is a danger of a declining inner city and work together to restore commerce and safe occupied buildings to ensure the vitality for the residents, businesses, and first responders.

Chapter 13:

Myths & Misconceptions in the Economic Development Debate

This chapter is composed of things we have heard from people we interviewed for the book, mostly from Haltom City, but also from other cities and states. Some of these appeared on Facebook in comments about business development. Most of these statements have been made by well-intentioned people who just don't understand business, the city's ordinances, the rules of commerce or just don't get how economic development really works.

Myth

1 **"There are too many car lots, gas stations, (pick any type of business) in town."**

Reality

In a free market, customers vote for the businesses they like by spending money on the goods and services they provide. If a gas station or car lot or any other kind of business stays open, it does so because enough people are signaling that they like and want it there by becoming customers. The rules of economics and commerce will determine how many of any given type of business is "too many." City council members and other politicians shouldn't be doing anything that limits competition. They should simply let markets work and let new and existing businesses compete for customers. Of course, they do have a duty to protect their citizens on health, safety, and objectionable issues like sexually oriented businesses.

Myth

2 **"A business is not hurt when it is made legal non-conforming."**

Reality

We have discussed this misconception at other places in this book, but it is an important one so we will answer it again here. A business that is made legal non-conforming can legally continue to operate, but it cannot expand, it cannot rebuild in the event of a fire or other disaster, and it loses the use if business operations must be suspended for a period of six months or more, for example. A buyer looking at a business that is operating as legal non-conforming will have pause because of these restrictions and he or she will certainly pay less for it than for the same business without the restrictions, so being made legal non-conforming certainly hurts the business owners who have been affected.

Myth

3 **"City leaders should discuss city business in private Facebook groups, rather than using their official pages."**

Reality

All city business should be discussed with maximum transparency. Discussing city business in private Facebook groups is a bad practice because not all voters are members of the group and not all voters get to see what a public official is saying about city business. In addition, city officials who comment as private citizens on city business do not have a duty to correct misstatements, the way they would if they were commenting in an official capacity. Citizens should expect transparency from public officials and private Facebook groups and pages are not transparent, especially when who moderates or controls the pages is not made clear.

Myth

4 **"Conditional use permits (CUPs) don't discourage businesses from starting."**

Reality

Those that believe this have never reviewed the CUP application and considered the hardship imposed by meeting all the requirements of the application or enduring months of public hearings just to find out what the conditions for the permit are. Many businesses must hire expensive consultants just to complete the processes. Certainly, many cities have CUP processes, Haltom City just imposes CUPs more frequently than nearby cities do placing it at a competitive disadvantage in the contest to attract small business startups. Many studies have shown that burdensome CUPs impede businesses from starting, as outlined in this book.

Myth

5 **"Citizens should be able to vote on which businesses they want."**

Reality

Other than sexually oriented businesses, health, safety, and other things like gambling, all businesses should be welcome as governed by zoning and permitted uses. That's what conditional use permits (CUPs) and special use permits (SUPs) are for. Public hearings impose the proper restrictions on unwanted businesses.

Myth

6 **"A major grocery store should come to Haltom City's central city."**

Reality

No large business is coming to a declining inner city, except maybe those that appeal to the lower demographic, like Dollar Stores or the new Ollie's. Even they are sensitive to declining corridors, the flight of customers, theft, crime, and drug use. Also, Haltom City has an Aldi, a smaller grocery store, which is all that can be supported right now. If the declining corridors became occupied again, with increased commerce, there could be a possibility of larger stores returning. They aren't interested in "lifting" an area, they want it already thriving.

Myth

7 "Business owners in HC who live elsewhere should not sit on any city committees because they don't live here and don't have anything to contribute to the community. If they cared about the city, they would live here."

Reality

This is a huge disconnect, and cities that don't recognize the importance of both landowners and business owners are losing a lot of potential brain power. City committees that relate to economic development should have at least one seat for a business owner that doesn't live in the city and a seat for one non-resident landowner. These stakeholders are a big part of the diversity needed to properly run a city.

Myth

8 "The city should only allow good businesses to open in a city."

Reality

The city should recognize that it is competing with nearby cities for small businesses. It should strive to have a table of uses that fairly places businesses in the proper zones based on intensity. It should consider how nearby cities treat businesses of a particular kind so that it can gain a comparative advantage by being just a little easier to open that kind of business than nearby cities are. It should resist substituting the judgement of politicians for the judgement of the marketplace when it comes to deciding if a business is good or bad.

Myth

9 **"Anyone wanting change in the city must have ulterior motives."**

Reality

Since the beginning of time activists have taken position on change. Without friction, change doesn't come, and activists on any side of a given issue don't have to have ulterior motives. Usually, ulterior motives are obvious to everyone. In most cases, detractors use such accusations as a smoke screen to try and dismiss comments from those that they don't like.

Myth

10 **"City leaders should protect existing businesses from new competitors."**

Reality

The city council's charge is not to limit competition. Local leaders should let free markets work.

Myth

11 "The firefighters don't want any more auto repair shops in Haltom City."

Reality

The firefighters, just like the council, should not be in the business of limiting competition. Just because the president of their PAC says they say they do not want more auto shops in Haltom City does not mean all firefighters feel that way.

Myth

12 "Car dealers were not made legal non-conforming in 2003 in Haltom City."

Reality

The city gave all dealers 6 months to come in and change to a new zoning category, an onerous and expensive process to those that didn't became legal non-conforming.

Myth

13 "It is too easy to open a car repair shop in Haltom City."

Reality

To the contrary, auto repair shops aren't allowed to open at all in any commercial zones, and only permitted in the industrial and heavy industrial zones of Haltom City after the applicant gets a CUP, a process that requires months of hearings and considerable expense. .

Myth

14 **"Because Haltom City has more auto repair shops per 1000 residents than surrounding cities, it must have too many."**

Reality

Haltom City had a brand as an automotive-oriented city. Ron Sturgeon can remember when the corridors were thriving with commerce in the 1980s and 1990s and believes those businesses left because of the city's changes directed at shutting them down. Auto repair shops can, of course, be ugly, but code enforcement should keep them compliant. If the city no longer wants automotive, which occupied as much as 25% of the businesses, the city should have a plan to attract other types of businesses to backfill the vacancy as automotive businesses shut down. Again, the city should not be in the business of limiting competition.

Myth

15 "Haltom United Business Alliance (HUBA) should work with city leaders. After all, we gave them what they asked for on the food trucks."

Reality

HUBA has repeatedly proposed changes that should be considered to bring more small business to Haltom City. Haltom City has never asked to work with the alliance and has not taken action on the alliance's proposals to bring more small businesses to the city or even recognized that the alliance exists.

Myth

16 "Haltom City is in decline, and it used to have a lot more automotive businesses. They didn't stop the decline from starting years ago so we really don't need them."

Reality

The decline of Haltom City is complex and involves many factors. HUBA has always said that it is too hard to open a business, which is causing increased vacancies over the last few decades. Most of that anti-business mantra is embodied in the use table, which requires many businesses to have public hearings, and restricting many business types to only the heavy commercial and industrial zones. Cities need almost all types of businesses.

Myth

17 "The city doesn't need any more title companies."

Reality

Cities shouldn't limit competition, and this comment is heard applying to all types of businesses that someone personally doesn't like. The council should not let personal dislikes guide which businesses come or leave.

Myth

18 "The city council needs to regulate how many sinks food trucks have in order to keep the public safe."

Reality

The city should not micro manage business plans, and in Haltom City's case, food trucks are regulated by the county just like restaurants. Also, such ordinances and controls should be worked out by the staff as part of new ordinance, not by a single or group of councilpersons.

Myth

19 "A mentoring program for small business owners who are faced with completing the CUP process won't really help open many small businesses. It's a waste of time by a special interest group with an agenda."

Reality

The business agenda for the business alliance is to bring more small businesses to the city. That should be a good thing for all stakeholders.

Myth

20 **"Ron Sturgeon backs the automotive businesses, the auto repair shops, because he makes money selling them parts from his junkyards. He is just doing it for the money."**

Reality

Ron hasn't owned a junkyard since he sold those he owned to Ford Motor Co. in 1999. He has no ulterior motives for his activist role in trying to bring more small businesses to Haltom City, no vacant buildings, no undeveloped land, and doesn't aspire to open or build in Haltom City.

Myth

21 **"The business alliance just wants to loosen up zoning in Haltom City so their members can start new businesses and run them in ways that are inconsiderate of their neighbors."**

Reality

Businesses that are non-compliant should be controlled by code enforcement. That said, yes, businesses are opened and run to make money, and almost universally it is good for the city and the residents. Very few if any businesses set out to be inconsiderate to their neighbors, and are unlikely to survive with that mantra.

Myth

22 **"Retail (brick and mortar) isn't in decline. It is not going away."**

Reality

Covid has accelerated the move to online for purchases. While they were shut in, people learned to buy more online and that's unlikely to decline measurably.

Myth

23 **"The reason Haltom City doesn't have a grocery store is all the auto shops and tire stores have crowded out other kinds of development."**

Reality

Grocery Stores come where there is enough need, also defined as revenue. Auto shops don't influence this, except to increase commerce, a good thing.

Myth

24 **"The city doesn't need any more strip centers."**

Reality

Again, commerce and private investment will determine how many there are, and they won't be built if there is no demand.

Myth

25 "Too much competition causes businesses to fail; we should have fewer so that they survive."

Reality

More businesses are almost always a good thing; competition is good. Revenues rise, the city collects more in taxes, and employment benefits.

Myth

26 "Cities should buy a property and then hold it so they can control the development using their money."

Reality

Cities should not try to control the economy or commerce. Private investment will guide what goes where, within reasonable zoning and use ordinances.

Myth

27 "We would rather have boarded up buildings than auto repair shops, body shops, quick lubes, tire stores and other automotive uses."

Reality

There are certainly some people in Haltom City who think this way, but city leaders need to think about what is in the interests of the city as a whole, rather than pandering to a vocal group of critics who want to write off a whole segment that has been a large part of the city's business community for decades.

Myth

28 **Tire stores are unattractive from the street because many of them store tires outside on racks. There isn't much that can be done except restricting them to the industrial and heavy industrial areas of town the way that Haltom City did in 2021.**

Reality

Some auto businesses are not the most aesthetically pleasing, however, a tire store is a retail business and should be allowed in the commercial parts of the city. HUBA suggested that Haltom City might want to revise its use matrix to have separate categories for tire store with outside display and tire store without outside display and that the city should allow those without outside display in most of the commercial zones and those with outside display in the heavier commercial zones that allow outside storage. Additionally, HUBA has asked Haltom City to change its ordinances to allow painted shipping containers that have been screened from view to be used for storage. If this were allowed, tire stores could store inventory in these containers in a way that would not be visible from the street. A lot can be done to solve these issues without banning a whole type of store from the commercial parts of Haltom City.

Chapter 14:

Numbers Tell a Story

Whether you are a member of a city council in a small city, a candidate for a similar office, or a voter concerned about decline in your city, you need to know how to use numbers to tell the story of your city. Throughout his time on City Council in Saint Leo, Florida, Gregory Smith used numbers extensively. As a serial entrepreneur, Ron Sturgeon is very comfortable with using numbers, metrics, and benchmarking to assess the performance of a venture, and has a book *Peer Benchmarking,* which is available on Amazon. As a founder and member of Haltom United Business Alliance (HUBA), Ron has used numbers in his presentations to Haltom City Council.

Both authors of this book have learned valuable lessons about using numbers that they will share in this final chapter.

- **Benchmark for population growth** – All cities want to grow, so benchmark your city against others in your area. Your brand or value proposition should draw them in. When they drive through your city, down the main drag, do they like what they see? Obviously, if there are more businesses and employment, there is likely to be population growth, people like to live close to work. In North Texas, there are about 1,000 people moving in every day, so the opportunity for growth is huge. Unfortunately, Haltom City has fallen from about the middle of the pack, out of 42 cities in Tarrant County, at #22 in year 2000, to #32 in 2019, according to census data. So, 75% of the cites in Tarrant County do a better job of attracting new residents. Ron believes that a lot of this decline is due to the city putting out its businesses unwelcome mat, especially for all the automotive businesses.

- **Benchmark your city against itself** – One way to use census and other data is to benchmark your city against itself over time. An important measure of prosperity is median household income. Here is census data showing median household income for Haltom City for the period 2000-2020.[28]

Census Year	Median Household Income	% Change
2000	$38,818	N/A
2010	$41,215	6.17%
2020	$52,709	27.89%

Population Growth

Name	Status	Population Census 4/1/1990	Population Census 4/1/2010	Growth 1990-2010	Rank	Population Census 4/1/2020	growth 2010-2020	Rank
Tarrant		1,170,103	1,809,034	154.60%		2,110,640	116.67%	
Texas		16,986,510	25,145,561	148.03%		29,145,505	115.91%	
Trophy Club	Town	4,030	8,026	199.16%	9	13,688	170.55%	1
Westlake	Town	404	994	246.04%	6	1,623	163.28%	2
Roanoke	City	1,893	5,962	314.95%	4	9,665	162.11%	3
Crowley	City	6,990	12,837	183.65%	10	18,070	140.76%	4
Edgecliff Village	Town	2,715	2,776	102.25%	38	3,788	136.46%	5
Pelican Bay	City	1,270	1,543	121.50%	24	2,049	132.79%	6
Burleson	City	16,296	36,876	226.29%	8	47,641	129.19%	7
Haslet	City	836	1,523	182.18%	11	1,952	128.17%	8
Mansfield	City	15,435	56,654	367.05%	3	72,602	128.15%	9
Kennedale	City	5,132	6,745	131.43%	21	8,517	126.27%	10
Fort Worth	City	448,560	744,800	166.04%	14	918,915	123.38%	11
Azle	City	9,307	10,860	116.69%	27	13,369	123.10%	12
Saginaw	City	8,548	20,048	234.53%	7	23,890	119.16%	13
Euless	City	38,225	51,263	134.11%	20	61,032	119.06%	14
Southlake	City	7,134	26,573	372.48%	2	31,265	117.66%	15
Flower Mound	Town	15,808	64,658	409.02%	1	75,956	117.47%	16
Sansom Park	City	3,927	4,679	119.15%	25	5,454	116.56%	17
Benbrook	City	19,523	21,203	108.61%	32	24,520	115.64%	18
Reno	City	2,387	2,491	104.36%	36	2,878	115.54%	19
Keller	City	13,673	39,627	289.82%	5	45,776	115.52%	20
Colleyville	City	12,638	22,809	180.48%	12	26,057	114.24%	21
White Settlement	City	15,477	16,116	104.13%	37	18,269	113.36%	22
Forest Hill	City	11,456	12,353	107.83%	33	13,955	112.97%	23
Grand Prairie	City	99,661	175,435	176.03%	13	196,100	111.78%	24
North Richland Hills	City	45,902	63,147	137.57%	19	69,917	110.72%	25
Richland Hills	City	8,008	7,787	97.24%	41	8,621	110.71%	26
Newark	City	613	1,000	163.13%	15	1,096	109.60%	27
Lakeside	Town	1,059	1,509	142.49%	17	1,649	109.28%	28
Grapevine	City	29,543	46,336	156.84%	16	50,631	109.27%	29
Haltom City	**City**	**32,775**	**42,566**	**129.87%**	**22**	**46,073**	**108.24%**	**30**
Hurst	City	33,435	37,344	111.69%	30	40,413	108.22%	31
Arlington	City	261,973	365,125	139.38%	18	394,266	107.98%	32
Pantego	Town	2,402	2,401	99.96%	40	2,568	106.96%	33
Bedford	City	43,768	46,990	107.36%	34	49,928	106.25%	34
Westworth Village	City	2,225	2,472	111.10%	31	2,585	104.57%	35
River Oaks	City	6,585	7,424	112.74%	28	7,646	102.99%	36
Everman	City	5,699	6,028	105.77%	35	6,154	102.09%	37
Halworthington Garde	City	1,756	2,259	128.64%	23	2,293	101.51%	38
Lake Worth	City	4,584	4,678	102.05%	39	4,711	100.71%	39
Watauga	City	20,005	23,497	117.46%	26	23,650	100.65%	40
Westover Hills	Town	672	639	95.09%	42	641	100.31%	41
Blue Mound	City	2,136	2,393	112.03%	29	2,393	100.00%	42
https://www.citypopulation.de/en/usa/texas/48439__tarrant/								

Haltom City has dropped from #22 to #40 compared to other Tarrant County cities.

- **Benchmark your city against nearby cities** – Another way to add additional context is to compare your city's numbers against those of nearby cities and your state. Below is median household income for Haltom City, North Richland Hills and Fort Worth from the censuses taken in 2010 and 2020.[29] As you can see, Haltom City's median household income has grown 20% less than Fort Worth's.

	Median Household Income		
	2020	2010	% Change
Fort Worth	$65,356	$48,224	35.53%
North Richland Hills	$71,076	$54,536	30.33%
Haltom City	$52,709	$41,215	27.89%

- **Pay attention to rankings** – Haltom City is one of 41 cities in Tarrant County. Looking at how Haltom City ranks against all the other cities in Tarrant County for median household income or another measure of prosperity can be an important way to add context. Adding context and specifics can help convince local policymakers to take constructive action to help turn the lights back on downtown. Below is a ranking of median household income for cities in Tarrant County for the year 2020.[30] Falling or rising rank on such a list can be an important indicator of the path that your city is on, and if you are keeping up with other cities.

Rank	City	Median Household Income
1	Westover Hills	$245,833
2	Southlake	$240,248
3	Westlake	$227,083
4	Colleyville	$163,509
5	Trophy Club	$147,477
6	Haslet	$142,656
7	Keller	$141,364
8	Flower Mound	$139,508
9	Dalworthington Gardens	$109,375
10	Mansfield	$105,182
11	Grapevine	$91,143
12	Lakeside	$85,917
13	Saginaw	$83,402
14	Burleson	$79,784
15	Kennedale	$77,763
16	Crowley	$76,720
17	Benbrook	$72,699
18	Azle	$72,614
19	Edgecliff Village	$72,143
20	Watauga	$71,897
21	North Richland Hills	$71,076
22	Bedford	$70,362
23	Grand Prairie	$66,097
24	Euless	$65,921
25	Fort Worth	$65,356
26	Hurst	$63,722
27	Richland Hills	$62,549
28	River Oaks	$62,326
29	Arlington	$61,176
30	Westworth Village	$60,227
31	Reno	$60,199
32	Lake Worth	$60,123
33	Blue Mound	$56,146
34	Pantego	$54,946
35	Newark	$54,792
36	Haltom City	$52,709
37	Sansom Park	$51,909
38	White Settlement	$48,996
39	Pelican Bay	$43,359
40	Everman	$43,352
41	Forest Hill	$41,496

- **Use appropriate metrics** – Some metrics are better than others for telling the story you need to tell. Below is a chart showing average earnings for the top 5% of earners for various places in Tarrant County. Although this illustration provides some insight into how top earners are faring, it may not be the best metric for really understanding how the bulk of your town is doing. If telling a story about the whole community is your goal, perhaps consider a broader metric.

- **Know the different key terms** – Whether you are a policymaker, a candidate, or a voter, you should invest the time to learn the vocabulary necessary to using numbers to tell stories about your city. The mean is the average of a set of data points. The median is the middle value in a set of values arranged from lowest to highest.

- **Know that some stories take a long time to unfold** – In 2003, Haltom City Council undertook a misguided effort to beautify the city by pushing out the small car dealers who were operating along NE 28th Street in Haltom City. The ordinance the City Council passed created a new zoning category for car dealers (C-5) and gave those who wanted the new zoning a set period of time to come in and apply for it. Few did and so most became legal non-conforming and were unable to improve their properties

Mean Household Income of the Top 5% by Place

Scope: households in Tarrant County, selected places in Tarrant County, and entities that contain Tarrant County

	$0M	$1M	%	#
Westlake		$1.6M	+351%	1
Westover Hls		$1.4M	+296%	2
Southlake		$1.2M	+222%	3
Colleyville		$0.8M	+112%	4
Dalworthington Gdns		$0.6M	+69.0%	5
Pecan Acres		$0.6M	+67.5%	6
Keller		$0.6M	+52.4%	7
Trophy Club		$0.5M	+49.7%	8
Briar		$0.5M	+47.5%	9
Flower Mound		$0.5M	+38.3%	10
Westworth Vlg		$0.5M	+30.1%	11
Grapevine		$0.4M	+19.4%	12
Dallas Area		$0.4M	+7.13%	
Pantego		$0.4M	+6.26%	13
Rendon		$0.4M	+1.34%	14
Mansfield		$0.4M	+0.27%	15
Tarrant		$0.4M	0%	
United States		$0.4M	-1.69%	
Texas		$0.4M	-2.13%	
Saginaw		$0.3M	-4.98%	16
West South Central		$0.3M	-7.77%	
South		$0.3M	-8.29%	
Fort Worth		$0.3M	-14.0%	17
N Richland Hls		$0.3M	-15.1%	18
Lakeside		$0.3M	-15.5%	19
Kennedale		$0.3M	-17.3%	20
Roanoke		$0.3M	-18.4%	21
Haslet		$0.3M	-18.5%	22
Hurst		$0.3M	-18.8%	23
Burleson		$0.3M	-21.5%	24
Arlington		$0.3M	-23.1%	25
Azle		$0.3M	-24.0%	26
Euless		$0.3M	-24.6%	27
Benbrook		$0.3M	-26.7%	28
Bedford		$0.3M	-27.6%	29
Newark		$0.2M	-34.0%	30
Grand Prairie		$0.2M	-35.1%	31
White Settlement		$0.2M	-35.9%	32
Reno		$0.2M	-36.1%	33
Watauga		$0.2M	-38.9%	34
Crowley		$0.2M	-39.4%	35
River Oaks		$0.2M	-39.4%	36
Haltom City		$0.2M	-41.4%	37
Everman		$0.2M	-42.4%	38
Edgecliff Vlg		$0.2M	-48.3%	39
Richland Hls		$0.2M	-51.7%	40
Pelican Bay		$0.2M	-52.5%	41
Lake Worth		$0.2M	-53.3%	42
Blue Mound		$0.2M	-54.5%	43
Forest Hill		$0.1M	-60.9%	44
Sansom Park		$0.1M	-65.9%	45

% percentage above or below mean household income of the top 5% of Tarrant County

rank of place out of 45 by mean household income of the top 5%

or expand if they were operating as car lots. Over the subsequent nearly two decades, the effects of that policy have worked themselves out as NE 28th Street has become an eyesore with many vacant properties that cannot be redeveloped for other purposes because they are platted as very small lots. The architects of the misguided effort are long gone, but the blight they created remains years later. It often takes a significant time for the effects of local policies, bad or good, to become clear. According to census data, transportation occupations dropped in Haltom City from 2013 to 2018 by 20%.

Numbers are an important tool in telling the story of your small city. Both Greg Smith and Ron Sturgeon wish you well in your efforts to tell your city's story in a compelling way so that you can help turn the lights back on Downtown.

Chapter 15:

Rebecca Boxall Shares
Her Ideas on Revitalization

Ron stumbled into this content when he asked Rebecca for an advance review of this book. He knew she was a change agent as a newly elected Arlington City Councilperson. Little did he know that she was working on the topic and had already been following the demise of inner cities and had even written a white paper containing her ideas to promote change.

Rebecca's career as an architect spans 30 years in Hawaii, Oregon and Texas. She has lived in Arlington since 2007 and is passionate about redevelopment, revitalization and elevating local communities.

Her district includes Downtown Arlington, University of Texas at Arlington and most of the older neighborhoods and industrial areas of the city.

Here are her thoughts:

1. **Small cities are uniquely positioned for the future in my opinion.** There is a lot written on this but in general the theory is that younger people, the millennials and generations after them, are looking for opportunities to start things from the ground up. Many are gravitating to smaller rust-belt cities where they have a better chance to have a say in local affairs and redevelop the city as they envision it. <u>Cities would be wise to market themselves to this age cohort.</u> This generation is less inclined than previous generations to work a standard 9-5 job. They want to be either their own boss or part of a small team of like-minded people with a common business goal. They also like to think of themselves as innovative rather than following older modes of business. One person I listen to a lot has described

Multi-tenant creative use of containers which appeals to millennials

them as seeking authenticity, which they think they can find, or create, in smaller venues. They have a lot of characteristics of business-minded recent immigrants.

2. **Smaller cities have an opportunity to change direction and reinvent themselves.** They have nothing to lose and a lot to gain by thinking outside the box. A commentator I listen to a lot, Chuck Mahron, of Strong Towns https://www.strongtowns.org/, writes a lot about small cities, particularly cities struggling or in decline. He advocates for what he calls "small bets" instead of chasing unicorns trying to lure big ventures to town. If you get a chance to look at the Strong Towns website, there is a lot of content there that fits right into what this book is about. In fact, I recommend you contact Chuck and have him come and speak to your mayor, city council and upper city management. He spoke at UTA a few years ago and was in Fort Worth last year for one of his "curbside chats." What he has to say is a real eye-opener. I highly recommend his book, *Strong Towns: A Bottom-Up Revolution to Rebuild American Prosperity.* One thing that Chuck does is illustrate that the most productive parts of your city are not always where you think they are. He does this with spike graphs that show each a map of the city parcel by parcel and how much it produces

in taxable income per square foot. The results are amazing.

3. **Since I've been on City Council in Arlington, I've come to realize how moribund the city policies and practices are, more so than I had already guessed.** It's probably the same in most cities, but in a smaller city like Haltom City, it should be easier to affect change.

4. **I have a lot of ideas about how cities or parts of cities can revitalize.** Most of them will require re-tooling of the zoning ordinances, as this book discusses. My district in Arlington has the oldest and some of the poorest areas. What I'm asking to be done is to create specific areas where the zoning ordinances are relaxed or changed to encourage redevelopment. I'm also advocating for pilot projects to demonstrate what can be done so it doesn't have to be a big change for the whole city. It's an uphill battle. Maybe Haltom City is a better place to try some of them out, who knows.

5. **I advocate for FAS (my own acronym).** Flexible-Adaptable-Scalable. If a project or redevelopment doesn't have at least two of these features, then it should not be considered. As you might imagine, zoning ordinances (and they are the same most everywhere) promote the very opposite of FAS. They

are rigid and very narrow in scope for each use type. There is no reason why many of these use types cannot be combined on a parcel or have the ability to change back and forth without a lot of red tape. The only thing holding this back is our rigid outdated zoning ordinances, which come from an era that is fast disappearing. They never really worked that well in the first place and it's depressing to think how much innovation was squashed because of ill-thought-out regulations.

6. **Bureaucracies get stuck in ways of doing things and hold onto them even if they are not working.** Due to rapid social changes, we are not likely to go back to businesses (or housing or anything else) the way we have thought of them in the past. The most open to change and nimbler cities will come out on top. This is another area where smaller cities have an advantage over medium or large cities.

White Paper
Incremental Up-Zoning Proposal
to Revitalize Our Cities

Rebecca Boxall, RA

One of the biggest obstacles to redevelopment is the time, cost, and hassle of getting a zoning change or

Creative use of shipping containers to appeal to young creative types. Haltom City doesn't allow use of shipping containers.

change-of-use-permit. This goes for every type of development from housing, commercial, to industrial areas.

Outdated zoning promotes single-use and often single-building type development or redevelopment. In city planning jargon this is referred to as Euclidean zoning. On most parcels there is no logical reason this has to be enforced. When an area is organically revitalized, it is often due to "urban pioneers" who are willing to live and work in areas that were previously thought undesirable. They are not bogged down by notions that they have to recreate exactly what was there before. Instead, they often combine or re-use building in a different way than what it was originally designed for. We've seen this over and over in countless cities where young creative types move into a less-desirable area and, over time, convert it into the hip place to be. There are countless examples of this. What lessons can we learn from this?

There is no reason why most land uses cannot be combined on the same site or sometimes in the same building. Euclidean zoning arbitrarily separated uses in the 1960s. At the time, this was thought of as modern and progressive planning. But it has had disastrous effects on our overall land use, not to mention encouraging more driving. Euclidean zoning has become so much the norm that people don't even realize there are other ways of land planning. Most zoning codes are based on this outdated zoning system, which has become so ubiquitous hardly anyone even questions it. When you ask why a code is written the way it is or what were they trying to achieve, often no one knows. It's simply that this is the way it's been done for decades. Because of this, we never get an opportunity to question whether the original goal is still valid today. The original intent is lost in time.

Even within the same use category there are further arbitrary separations. Where this is most apparent is in housing. Under old zoning, housing is separated by lot size, house size, housing design/materials, etc. In more recent times, there is even separate zoning for age of residents. The same thing has happened in the commercial sector. Whole sections of towns are designated for a small subset of use types that, for the most part, do not require separation.

My contention is that cities would benefit from less-rigid land planning and allow for creative, innovative developments, with less red tape. We should at least try the theory out in small sections of cities. Sometimes this is done off the books in what is called guerilla urbanism or tactical urbanism, whereby people will run two businesses out of one storefront or put in an additional use that they do not have a certificate of occupancy for. But we could allow this to occur, by right. Many cities do have a provision for accessory uses, but staff is usually afraid to allow it even though they have the authority to make those administrative decisions. It's just easier to say no.

Proposal: Allow incremental up-zoning and/or use combinations *by right*--meaning that the property owner or developer would not have as much red tape to navigate--in specific areas of cities in need of revitalization. These would be living labs. Here are some ideas how to implement this:

- Choose an area to start on: maybe a segment of road or apply to a broader category such as along any road larger than two lanes

- Allow an incremental jump in zoning category (or combination of the existing use and one other use) *by right*

- Reduce parking minimums (say by 10%), or give administrative authority to use occupiable space rather than total square feet in the calculation

- Reduce setbacks and/or lot coverage minimums or increase height allowance

- Create a form pattern book (What does your city want to see physically (instead of concentrating on uses, concentrate on form, appearance, etc.) as a guideline? This helps developers and designers have a springboard from which to work. Be descriptive, not prescriptive. Concentrate on what you want, not what you don't want for your city. This involves really thinking about what you are trying to achieve and developing a rationale for it.)

A building use does not necessarily mean it has to be a certain form, particularly if it has more than one use. Don't get bogged down into thinking of a certain use having to look a certain way. Any use can be attractive and add to the overall character you are trying to achieve.

In residential-zoned properties along arterial or collector roads, allow incremental up-zoning to the next notch of zoning category with the minimum to be the lowest multi-family zone. Allow mixed-use residential, plus at least one other use such as a dwelling unit above or on the same site. This creates transition zones between housing types rather than exclude them altogether. (Allow doesn't mean the property owner can only redevelop the lot into higher density, it simply means they are allowed to).

These strategies incentivize redevelopment and creativity. The flexibility adds unrealized value to the property. The owner has to take advantage of it before it pays off. This gets around the complaint of picking and choosing winners, or gentrifying. At the same time, it gives a property owner potential additional equity that can be used to secure a loan based on increased revenue. It also minimizes the perceived risk from the lender's perspective, since they know at least that the red tape will not be an obstacle. These measures allow local property owners to invest in their property for greater returns; therefore, less likely to sell out to land consolidators or speculators, which helps keep local money local.

We are moving into an area of fast social and business change. There is a lot of uncertainty, and Covid has exacerbated and accelerated change. The more flexibility we build into our ordinances, the more easily we will be able to weather changes. The more flexible and adaptable (and I would argue scalable) something is, the less fragile it is. This is the true meaning of sustainability. Some cities are going to figure this out sooner than others and reap the benefits.

Cities are kinetic. They are constantly changing to meet new conditions, new ways of doing things, new generations, new technology, and unexpected events. Let's get our ordinances to work within that reality rather than in futile opposition to it. An example of a new use category coming into being is co-warehousing and is discussed more in the July 2019 online article by Colliers Knowledge Leader, "Co-Warehousing: The Next Big Thing in Distribution?". Similar to co-office space, this concept allows small businesses that need space for inventory but don't need enough to rent warehouse space, plus buy forklifts and other equipment. This allows shar-

Example of a multi-use building, with residential, medical, office and a residence, LI bldg.-Bankroft Light industrial building, Berkeley project. Photo credit to Billy Hustace Photography.

ing of equipment and smaller increments of storage space that can quickly fluctuate (more or less space without the hassle of releasing, moving, etc.)

An example of adding a different use on a light industrial site such as a car lot or auto repair shop, add a pop-up café in front in the parking lot that would add street appeal and give customers somewhere to wait. Sublease it to a person who wants to start a small business but doesn't have the ability to pay high rent and improvements in a commercial strip. This helps both businesses, and it improves the streetscape. Win, win, win. There are unlimited ideas that could come into being if not for onerous zoning ordinances.

Other articles of interest

10 Reasons Millennials are Moving to Small Towns
https://www.sparefoot.com/self-storage/blog/22586-
10-reasons-millennials-moving-small-towns/
amp/

Where Did All the Small Developers Go?
https://www.strongtowns.org/journal/2021/10/18/
where-did-all-the-small-developers-go
You'd be forgiven for thinking that what produced these places must have been enlightened, careful planning; keen aesthetic sensibilities; a highly ordered process. Actually, what produced them was the opposite: a highly decentralized process in which people did what worked and had been proven to work, and they did it over and over and over again.

Why millennials are flocking to Rust Belt real estate
https://www.cnbc.com/2018/09/23/why-millennials-
are-flocking-to-rust-belt-real-estate.html
Rather than just home ownership, "it is about having roots and contributing to the revival of a place that needs businesses that create jobs and create value."

Gen Z Renters Flocking to Smaller Towns in Midwest, South
https://www.globest.com/2021/02/22/gen-z-renters-
flocking-to-smaller-towns-in-midwest-south/?slre-
turn=20220001154639

Millennials Could Be a Boon to Smaller Communities. How Can Those Towns Attract Younger Workers?

https://www.route-fifty.com/management/2020/08/ millennials-smaller-communities-attract-younger-workers/168084/

Millennials can play a major role in revitalizing America's small communities, but small towns can't wait for an influx that might never come. By spending money wisely to create attractive opportunities for these younger workers, states and municipalities can begin to transform small towns into hotbeds of creativity, economic vigor and community. Building a plan like this for millennials can serve as a guide for a long-term talent pipeline to attract future generations, like Generation Z and beyond.

What I've Learned from Working with Gen Z Entrepreneurs

https://www.worth.com/gen-z-entrepreneurs/

Gen Z is rapidly becoming known as the most entrepreneurial generation ever, with 62 percent of Gen Zers indicating they have started—or intend to start—their own business. And those who have already started down this path are not only embracing entrepreneurship but also transforming it with unique approaches to brand building, upskilling and operations.

Epilogue and Haltom City Concept Plan

Epilogue

I set out to write this book after it recently took me over 12 months to get permission with new rules to open a very straightforward business in Haltom City, an event center.

I started my first of many businesses in Haltom City 50 years ago. I raised my family in Haltom City, in Skyline Mobile Home Park where I got my first rental property by upgrading to a double wide and renting my single wide. I love small businesses, and found success in the auto salvage business which I later sold to Ford Motor Co.

Since then, I've watched as the city steadily declined. I knew something wasn't quite right but wasn't sure what. I founded a business alliance in the city in 2020 and discovered the first clue to what was part of the problem. The city council wouldn't even acknowledge the alliance, much less discuss any ideas the business community had for bringing more businesses to the city. They even said they didn't want competition for existing businesses.

Their public workshops on new ordinances usually didn't allow the public to even speak. And they passed ordinances essentially putting over 200 automotive businesses on the "do-not-want list" with rules to phase them out. They made it clear that business owners didn't have a seat at the table unless they lived in the city. I saw that as a huge disconnect. Then I started doing the research you have read in this book. I was shocked, as it became abundantly clear that decades of neglect for the business community was at least partly to blame for the boarded-up buildings. I also networked with others studying the same topic, and connected with Rebecca Boxall, an innovative architect and change agent for her district serving on the council, with some of the oldest parts of Arlington.

Then when I got the empirical data, it told the whole story. While DFW enjoys 1,000 people per day moving into the area, Haltom City fell from the halfway point to the bottom 25% in population growth. The demographics were stalled as compared to sister cities.

More research found other cities with the same issues but with lots of success stories and documented and tested ideas to bring change. I am not alone! Early reviews of this book, many from public officials reinforce my belief that a strong relationship with the business community is the foundation for improvement.

Now, I am on a mission—to save my city, the one that gave me more than one opportunity to become a serial entrepreneur. I started homeless and broke after my dad died when I was in high school, and I'm one of those that believes the American dream is still alive, though the barriers to entry may be daunting in Haltom City. I'm in the fall of my life, with clean hands and no conflicts of interest, and have the time and the money to try to make Haltom City great again.

I know it's a daunting task. It's going to take many election cycles to get a progressive business-friendly city council. I hope you have learned something in these pages and are motivated to be a change agent in your city. Onward and upward.

R.S.

A Concept Plan for Haltom City

In business, we often find that plans, ideas and new policies are sometimes expedited when someone is charged with presenting a concept plan. This skips past committees, departments, etc. grinding along producing, sometimes painfully, a concept plan. The good thing about a concept plan is that it gets folks talking, and creative juices flowing, including those for, and those against. Don't like some portion of it? That's great, as part of the collaborative process – make an alternative suggestion that improves on the original one. I love the thought that a concept plan could embrace attracting millennials to the city. I think that concept along with a new plan that looks like an incubator for startups and entrepreneurs, bolstered with real reductions in the barriers to entry could be so exciting. Such a plan would also require less marketing, if it was innovative enough, with a little push in marketing, it would be picked up by the media and written about time and again. Talk about an economic engine! It might even include micro grants to help start-ups. I had proposed to another city to advise on bringing a starter home (below $200,000) community built with shipping containers. This would leverage on my rare experience when I recently constructed a business park with 150 containers, or my new 3 story home built with containers. What a centerpiece for the marketing of the "new" Haltom City! I am not interested in residential development but could advise at no cost.

I will start the ball rolling, you can discard all of it or portions, and please add to it, but think about it, and talk to others. One thing is a certainty, without a plan nothing is going to change.

- Consider hiring a consultant (not an engineering firm) to make a proposal after some amount of review of where the city is and where it would like to be. It would be great if the city considered strong-towns.org for that help, as they have helped a lot of cities that are wanting to be bring revitalization. I had committed to $250,000 to help bring a grocery store, but perhaps a portion of that could be earmarked to reimburse the city for consulting expenses. It's a great way to show my sincere interest in this effort as well. The Strong Towns people specialize in such consulting work, visit their website www.Strongtowns.org for more info.

- Identify the parts of town that need help, and that are different, and agree on what the differences are.

- Come up with a brand for the city that can be achieved. Proud and Progressive was a good one, but I'm not married to it.

- Create a district, perhaps south of Broadway, to use reduced requirements for occupancies and development.

- Decide on a plan to make it easier for businesses to start, by modifying the use matrix, eliminating a lot of the permitted uses/hearings.

- Consider a top to bottom rewrite of the ordinances, as outlined in Boxall's concept.

- Streamline Occupancy permits and Change of Use requirements.

- Make automobile uses, including dealers allowed in heavier C and M zones, only requiring a CUP in lighter C zones. (This could exclude the areas outside the zone.)

- Create a new annual fee and license for automotive businesses, $100 annually, with 6-month inspections for compliance. The fee would cover the costs of inspections. This would help keep these uses looking good, and an asset to the city.

- Track inquiries and follow up with those that inquire as to why they did or didn't come (or buy property) and if they need help understanding any requirements.

- Determine how many opportunities there are to bring new businesses with this tracking.

- Create financial incentive plans to get new tenants in any building vacant for a year or more, with money for façade, grounds or tenant improvement, matching $1 from city for each $3 spent by owner or tenant up to $25,000 from the city per building.

- Review the sign ordinances to make them simpler and streamline the process, and allow signs on more than one side of a building when the adjacent properties are not residential.

- Count the vacant buildings in the district, once annually, and generate a report on progress to increase occupancy.

- Define other metrics to track efforts.

- Add an ordinance that allows one business or property owner to serve on any board, panel, commission or elected position, regardless of where they live, so long as that representation doesn't exceed 20% of the panel.

- Start a mantra of getting everyone thinking about how to make it easier to nurture new and existing businesses, and to train city employees to think outside the box. Empower them to make decisions that make sense to accomplish the goal. Most of them don't realize they are thinking in the box, they are just doing what they've learned to do, and they don't know any other way to do their job.

- Make sure the city manager is capable of leading others through all the imminent issues, and is bought into the value of small business growth within the city, and that he has a positive attitude that he can convey to others, while he empowers them. It's a business lesson that many city managers simply can't comprehend. The typical city manager will be more experienced with the bureaucracy of covering everyone's rear end, and wont understand the trade off of lowering everything to the lowest common denominator, protecting the citizenry vs the barriers that those rules or actions create for others.

- What else?

In any case, an idea without a plan or date is a dream, so let's get moving making Haltom City the once proud city with bustling corridors it once was.

Visit www.MakeHaltomCityGreatAgain.com
for information on the book and updates.

References

1 The Evolution of Rome. 2021. The Timeline. [online] Available at: <https://romabyrachel.weebly.com/the-timeline.html> [Accessed 22 December 2021].

2 "Profile of General Population and Housing Characteristics: 2010 Demographic Profile Data (DP-1): Haltom City, Texas". United States Census Bureau.

3 Frequently Asked Questions about Small Business. (2012). https://www.sba.gov/sites/default/files/FAQ_Sept_2012.pdf

4 Another Major Chain Store Closes, Leaving Haltom City's Inner City Another Vacancy. (n.d.). 24-7 Press Release Newswire. Retrieved December 22, 2021, from https://www.24-7pressrelease.com/press-release/487092/another-major-chain-store-closes-leaving-haltom-citys-inner-city-another-vacanc

5 The Coca-Cola Company. (2017). The Coca-Cola Company. https://www.coca-colacompany.com

6 City Council Member Salary. (n.d.). Comparably. Retrieved December 22, 2021, from https://www.comparably.com/salaries/salaries-for-city-council-member

7 City Manager Salary | PayScale. (n.d.). Www.payscale.com. https://www.payscale.com/research/US/Job=City_Manager/Salary

8 VILLAGE OF EUCLID V. AMBLER REALTY CO. (2018, May 12). Encyclopedia of Cleveland History | Case Western Reserve University. https://case.edu/ech/articles/v/village-euclid-v-ambler-realty-co

9 Haltom City, Texas | Official Website - Zoning Map. (n.d.). Www.haltomcitytx.com. Retrieved December 23, 2021, from https://www.haltomcitytx.com/maps-planning-community-development/haltom-city-zoning-map

10 Municode Library. (n.d.). Library.municode.com. Retrieved December 23, 2021, from https://library.municode.com/tx/haltom_city/codes/code_of_ordinances

11 Haltom City, Texas | Official Website - Tax Increment Reinvestment Zone Board. (n.d.). Www.haltomcitytx.com. Retrieved December 23, 2021, from https://www.haltomcitytx.com/tax-increment-rein-

vestment-zone-board/1436-haltom-city-tax-increment-reinvest-ment-zone-board

12 How Does A Tax Base Grow? (n.d.). Www.amarilloedc.com. Retrieved December 23, 2021, from https://www.amarilloedc.com/blog/how-does-a-tax-base-grow

13 Ibid.

14 Ibid.

15 Ibid.

16 What Cities Should Be Doing for Small Business. (2016, November 4). Governing. https://www.governing.com/gov-institute/voices/col-cities-focus-economic-development-job-strategies-small-business.html

17 Kenton, W. (2020, March 27). Brand. Investopedia. https://www.investopedia.com/terms/b/brand.asp

18 City Branding | Case Studies and Examples | TPBO. (2019, August 23). https://placebrandobserver.com/city-branding-explained/

19 ThemeGrill. (2015, January 26). 5-Step Approach to Place Branding: Guide for Place Developers and Brand Managers | The Place Brand Observer. Placebrandobserver.com. https://placebrandob-server.com/five-step-place-branding-approach/

20 Ibid.

21 Murphy, M. (n.d.). A Private Sector Model for Rebuilding Inner-city Competitiveness: Lessons from MidTown Cleveland. Brookings. Retrieved December 23, 2021, from https://www.brookings.edu/research/a-private-sector-model-for-rebuilding-inner-city-competi-tiveness-lessons-from-midtown-cleveland/

22 The Competitive Advantage of the Inner City. (1995, May). Harvard Business Review. https://hbr.org/1995/05/the-competitive-advantage-of-the-inner-city

23 Murphy, M. (n.d.). A Private Sector Model for Rebuilding Inner-city Competitiveness: Lessons from MidTown Cleveland. Brookings. https://www.brookings.edu/research/a-private-sector-model-for-re-building-inner-city-competitiveness-lessons-from-midtown-cleve-land/

24 Murphy, M. (n.d.). A Private Sector Model for Rebuilding Inner-city Competitiveness: Lessons from MidTown Cleveland. Brookings.

https://www.brookings.edu/research/a-private-sector-model-for-re-building-inner-city-competitiveness-lessons-from-midtown-cleve-land/

25 In Baltimore and Cleveland, a unique approach to reviving the inner city. (2015, May 1). Grist. https://grist.org/living/in-baltimore-and-cleveland-a-unique-approach-to-reviving-the-inner-city/

26 Urban Decentralization and Income Inequality - Federal ...https://files.stlouisfed.org › 2008/01 › Wheeler PDF

27 Ibid.

28 United States Census Bureau. (n.d.). Explore Census Data. Explore 2020 Census Data. Retrieved January 1, 2022, from https://data.census.gov/cedsci/

29 Ibid.

30 Ibid.

31 Steele, J. [Jayson Steele]. (2021, December). Haltom City has been in decline for decades. [Online Forum Post]. Facebook.

About the Author
Ron Sturgeon

Ron Sturgeon is a classic American entrepreneur. His rags-to-riches story began when, at the age of 17, he launched his own auto salvage business after his dad died and he had no money and no place to live. He went on to build it into one of the largest operations of its kind in the United States.

In 1999, he sold his chain of salvage yards to Ford Motor Company. He repurchased what had become a money-losing business from Ford several years later. After returning it to profitability, Sturgeon and three partners sold it once more to Schnitzer Industries.

Today Sturgeon is a successful real estate investor and founder of Mr. Mission Possible small business consulting. He is also the founder of the DFW Elite Toy Museum.

Sturgeon has published nine popular business books, two are in reprint, and several have been printed in other languages.

About the Author
Gregory Smith

Gregory Smith lives in Florida with his wife of 51 years. He holds a Master of Business Administration with a concentration in Quality Management from Wayne State University. In the course of his career, he served on the Utilities Committee for Southfield 2000, a long-term planning project for the City of Southfield, Michigan, a city of 75,000 people at that time. He also served on a commission examining fair housing issues for the same municipality. He successfully helped automotive suppliers in the Detroit area build viable quality management systems to reduce costs while improving product quality. His experience includes eleven years in regulatory and government affairs for Michigan Bell.

In 1992, he was recognized for his contributions to The Mayor's Committee for the 21st Century, organized to help avert a downgrade in the bond rating for the City of Detroit. Later, he served multiple terms of elective office at the municipal level in Florida.

ALSO BY RON STURGEON

Mr. Mission Possible Magazine

409 Low-Cost Events (with Linda Allen)

Getting to Yes with your Banker

Peer Benchmarking Groups

Green Weenies and Due Diligence

How to Salvage Millions From Your Small Business

How to Salvage More Millions From Your Small Business

*The Insider's Guide to Earning 100k
as a Self-Employed Salon Pro*

*Homeless to 100 Million: An Entrepreneur's
Roadmap to Building Wealth*

Order them on Amazon or at MrMissionPossible.com!